Praise for The Contrarian's Guide to Leadership

"Real thought and leadership run everywhere in this distillation from Steve Sample's rich experience as a leader. He writes easily and well, but the points he makes run deep and help you reflect on your own experience. Read this book at your own risk: you just might learn something startling."

—*George P. Shultz, former U.S. Secretary of State*

"Every leader or anyone who hopes to be one should read what Steven Sample says about leadership. No one could possibly say it better than he has in *The Contrarian's Guide to Leadership*. This gem of focused wisdom is presented with such amazing originality, clarity, and artful eloquence that it often holds the reader spellbound. It is sure to become *the* classic leadership text."

—*Simon Ramo, cofounder, TRW Inc.*

"This is an intoxicating read, a bushwhacker's delight. With swift, sure strokes, Steve Sample cuts down a lot of bad ideas about leadership and opens up a new path for the next generation to follow. No wonder he has turned around not one but two major universities!"

—*David Gergen, noted commentator, best-selling author, and adviser to four U.S. presidents*

"*The Contrarian's Guide to Leadership* is a unique guide to effective management because it's written by someone who practices what he preaches. Steven Sample isn't someone who just writes about leadership; he leads. As a result, he offers us fascinating reading, illuminating a way that others may follow."

—*Michael Eisner, chairman and chief executive officer, the Walt Disney Company*

"I loved this book attributing the huge recent gains at USC to a learnable, determined rationality that especially values correct decisions that are contrary to conventional wisdom."

—*Charles Munger, vice chairman, Berkshire Hathaway Inc.*

"This splendid work, unlike other recent textbooks and cookbooks on leadership, explores the issues and values that are the essential foundation of leadership. Enlivened with practical examples and enriched by personal experience, this is a book of major stature and enduring significance."

—*Frank Rhodes, president emeritus, Cornell University*

"In this era of hype and simplistic how-to lists, Steven Sample's refreshing book stands out for its depth and unusual personal insight. Lessons from great leaders of history blend with his experience as university president to illustrate the many roles leaders play, from artful listener to entertaining storyteller, as they struggle with circumstances en route to significant accomplishments. Reading this provocative book will help all leaders better understand themselves and their choices."

—*Rosabeth Moss Kanter,*
Arbuckle Professor of Business Administration,
Harvard Business School, and best-selling author of Evolve:
Succeeding in the Digital Culture of Tomorrow

"Steven Sample goes well beyond conventional wisdom about the art of leadership and brings a totally new dimension to the rich body of literature on the topic, dotting this lively narrative with pearls of wisdom and insight based on his wealth of experience. What emerges is a stimulating and provocative 21st century vision for how leadership can be taught, learned, and practiced."

—*Ray Irani, chairman and chief executive officer,*
Occidental Petroleum Corp.

"*The Contrarian's Guide to Leadership* is not only a helpful guide to effective leadership; it is a thoughtful guide to successful living. One main point that comes through is that 'big-time' leadership is only possible after answering tough and probing questions about one's own skills and values. In this, there are no fail-safe equations for leadership. For a big-time leader, character carries the day."

—*Dianne Feinstein, U.S. senator*

Warren Bennis (signature)

A WARREN BENNIS BOOK

This collection of books is devoted exclusively to new and exemplary contributions to management thought and practice. The books in this series are addressed to thoughtful leaders, executives, and managers of all organizations who are struggling with and committed to responsible change. My hope and goal is to spark new intellectual capital by sharing ideas positioned at an angle to conventional thought—in short, to publish books that disturb the present in the service of a better future.

Books in the Warren Bennis Signature Series

Branden,
Self-Esteem at Work

Mitroff/Denton,
A Spiritual Audit of Corporate America

Schein,
The Corporate Culture Survival Guide

Sample,
The Contrarian's Guide to Leadership

Lawrence/Nohria,
Driven

the **Contrarian's** Guide to Leadership

Steven B. Sample

Foreword by
Warren Bennis

JOSSEY-BASS
A Wiley Imprint
www.josseybass.com

FIRST PAPERBACK EDITION PUBLISHED IN 2003.

Published by Jossey-Bass
A Wiley Imprint
989 Market Street, San Francisco, CA 94103-1741   www.josseybass.com

Jossey-Bass books and products are available through most bookstores. To contact Jossey-Bass directly call our Customer Care Department within the U.S. at 800-956-7739, outside the U.S. at 317-572-3986, or fax 317-572-4002.

Jossey-Bass also publishes its books in a variety of electronic formats. Some content that appears in print may not be available in electronic books.

Library of Congress Cataloging-in-Publication Data

Sample, Steven B., 1940-
The contrarian's guide to leadership / Steven B. Sample; foreword by Warren Bennis.-1st ed.
    p. cm.
  Includes bibliographical references.
   ISBN 0-7879-5587-6 (alk. paper)
   ISBN 0-7879-6707-6 (pbk.)
   1. Leadership. I. Title.
HD57.7 .S255 2002
303.3'4-dc21   2001003576

Printed in the United States of America
FIRST EDITION
HB Printing   10 9 8 7 6 5 4
PB Printing   10 9 8

Contents

To Kathryn—

the light of my life and love of my heart

Foreword

There are few originals left in American society today—men and women who speak with a unique voice and who can offer an unconventional perspective and bracing authenticity. Steve Sample is an undisputed original. Simply put, his is a voice that should be heard by all those who would aspire to lead thoughtfully and effectively in our own time. *The Contrarian's Guide to Leadership* is Steve's effort to create a leadership manual for such people—and it has the look of a classic.

This is among the rarest of contemporary leadership books: a rigorously honest one that is both brutally unsentimental and firmly grounded morally. Its lessons and insights are more given to raising difficult questions than offering simple answers. And at a time in which many might want to believe that mere good intentions can win the day, this book reminds us that true leadership is a demanding vocation that requires would-be leaders to summon that which is best and strongest within themselves.

Just as this is a rare book, the author is a rare person: a technologist with an unusual passion for the arts and humanities and a spectacularly successful practitioner of leadership who imparts his wisdom easily to others. I would wager there is not another person alive who could have written the book in your hands, which is a profound weaving together of great truths about human beings, society, art, science and technology, and any other topic under the sun.

My own experience with Steve Sample goes back to when I helped recruit him to the presidency of USC more than a decade ago, when it was clear that he was a leader's leader. Since then, we've shared a marvelous experience coteaching an undergraduate course for upperclassmen entitled "The Art and Adventure of Leadership." I quickly realized that what Steve was teaching wasn't being said in the management textbooks and popular literature of our day. What he has to say is so fresh, yet paradoxically so timeless, so at-an-angle to conventional wisdom, that this book will instantly be recognized as an invaluable addition to the literature on leadership.

No manner of leader, save possibly a mayor of a large city, deals with as vast and complicated a cartography of stakeholders as does the head of a major American research university. Speaking from personal experience, I can say that a university president is called on to be an entertainer, a visionary, a priest, a psychologist, and a CEO of ten or twenty vastly different enterprises gathered under the seal of one university.

With that, it's obvious that leaders in other realms have a great deal that they can learn from an effective university president, and Steve is the best—perhaps one of the two or three best of the past half-century. No other university president I'm aware of has been able to take on not one but two very different universities—a public East Coast university and a private West Coast university, each with its own deeply rooted tendencies and traditions—and help each one move significantly closer to the fulfillment of its enormous potential.

Steve has in particular shown an unusual ability to "evangelize the future" to a dizzying array of stakeholders. At USC, he's led his myriad constituencies to enroll enthusiastically in a lofty dream of what they could accomplish together. Even more impressive, the results—which include a doubling in the number of applications from high school students, a dramatic 240-point rise in

SAT scores for incoming freshmen, the establishment of pioneering research institutes, the development of a unique undergraduate curriculum, and the smashing of national fundraising records—show that he has been able to *mobilize* those constituencies to follow through with the work and the sacrifices necessary to attain this shared dream. His success was reflected in *Time* magazine's selection of USC as College of the Year 2000, and by a widespread view that USC is doing nothing less than redefining the concept of the American university for the twenty-first century.

Steve is an astute student of history and a good storyteller, offering meaningful lessons from his personal life, his career, and the lives of great leaders of every age. His single greatest contribution to the discussion of leadership is his ability to fix a person's mind squarely on the agonies of leadership, the unavoidable "hurtin' decisions" that have kept a Harry Truman, a Thomas More, a Margaret Thatcher or the corner drugstore manager awake at four o'clock in the morning.

While many long for a roseate leadership style that can rally institutions and persons without the threat of pain or burden, Steve argues persuasively in this book that there is always a likelihood of casualties and that a great leader must be willing to count up the cost of any noble vision or bold action. His lessons have a colorful, urgent, even impatient quality, and they prompt considerable reflection and soul-searching. They are relevant for everyone.

I wouldn't at all be surprised to see this book become the first of a series of reflections by a leader who has looked deeply inside himself and his world and allowed the result to be of value to others. But while waiting for future works to come forth from Steve, there are enormous riches to be mined here in this volume. May you be confounded and delighted by what you encounter in the following pages.

Santa Monica, California   Warren Bennis
August 2001

Acknowledgments

First of all I should like to acknowledge the tremendous debt I owe to my friend and colleague Warren Bennis. It was he who, as chairman of USC's presidential search committee, was instrumental in recruiting Kathryn and me to USC in 1991. It was he who persuaded me, a professor of electrical engineering, to co-teach with him a course in leadership for juniors and seniors; this course has proven over the past six years to be one of the best learning experiences of my life. And it was Warren, world-famous author of some twenty-seven books on leadership, who ultimately convinced me to undertake writing *The Contrarian's Guide to Leadership* and who continued to advise and encourage me at every step of the way.

I also want to thank Rob Asghar, a former USC colleague and now an independent writer and editor, for investing so much of his time in helping me sit down and actually *write* this book. Engineers and scientists are not accustomed to writing pages and pages of straight text. When we write books in our scientific fields, we first lay out all the equations, graphs, charts, illustrations and tables that will form the meat of the book, and then knit these technical pieces together with a bit of text here and there. So for me to write nearly three hundred typewritten pages of pure narrative was extraordinarily difficult, and I would never have gotten it done without Rob's persistent handholding, creative ideas and brilliant editorial skills.

Next on my list of people to thank is Martha Harris, USC's vice president for public relations and a good personal friend. Martha believed from the outset that my contrarian ideas made good sense, and that they could and should be woven together into a coherent whole. She, along with Rob Asghar, deserves tremendous credit for holding my feet to the fire during the many months it took to write this book, and for critiquing numerous drafts of the text as it evolved.

I've dedicated this book to my wife Kathryn, who for over forty years has been my best friend and the most important person in my life. Kathryn was a principal reader, critic and sounding board for this entire project. She also constantly encouraged me throughout the writing of this book, as did my daughter Michelle Smith and her husband Kirk, my daughter Elizabeth Sample, my mother-in-law (and good friend) Evelyn Brunkow, and my grandchildren, Katherine Smith and Andrew Smith.

Special thanks are due the students in Warren's and my leadership class for providing me with extraordinary and exciting insights into leaders and leadership. Thanks are also due the assistant lecturers who made this course such a tremendous success, including especially Elizabeth Bleicher, Athena Perrakis, Cleve Stevens, Rich Fortenberry and Ken Graham.

My colleagues in the President's Office have gone out of their way to be supportive of this project, even when it made their own jobs more difficult. So I wish to thank all of them, and most especially Anne Westfall, Martie Steggell, Jan Popkoff, Sherri Sammon, and Laureen Morita.

Each of us has had teachers and mentors who have played crucial roles in helping us become who we are, and to whom we are indebted beyond words. My list of such people includes Howard Sample, Dorothy Hatch, M. E. Van Valkenburg, Fred Brunkow, Howard H. Sample, Sam Regenstrief, John Hicks, Harry Williams, D. B. Varner, the members of the Council of the University at

Buffalo, the trustees of the University of Southern California, and many others. I've also had the privilege of growing and growing up as a leader under the tutelage of scores of my administrative and faculty colleagues at Purdue, Nebraska, UB and USC, including especially Lloyd Armstrong, Dennis Dougherty, Alan Kreditor, Jane Pisano, Steve Ryan, Bill Greiner, Bob Wagner, Ron Stein, Hans Brisch and Gene Trani.

Finally I want to thank my book agent, Caroline O'Connell, for helping me have the luxury of a book contract in hand *before* I started writing, and Susan Williams and all the people at the Jossey-Bass division of John Wiley & Sons for their patience, understanding, and support.

About the Author

Steven B. Sample became the tenth president of the University of Southern California in March 1991. Sample is an electrical engineer, a musician, an outdoorsman, a professor, and an inventor. In 1998 he was elected to the National Academy of Engineering for his contributions to consumer electronics and leadership in interdisciplinary research and education. He regularly teaches undergraduate courses at USC while serving as president.

Under Sample's leadership, USC has become world-renowned in the fields of communication and multimedia technologies, has received national recognition for its innovative community partnerships, and has solidified its status as one of the nation's leading research universities. The unique character of USC's undergraduate programs has been widely acclaimed in recent years.

Sample is the author of numerous journal articles and published papers in science and engineering and higher education. His patents in the field of digital appliance controls have been licensed to practically every major manufacturer of microwave ovens in the world; over 200 million home appliances have been built using his inventions.

Sample came to USC from the State University of New York at Buffalo. During his tenure there, SUNY-Buffalo became the first public university in New York or New England to be elected to membership in the prestigious Association of American Universities.

the **Contrarian's**
Guide to
Leadership

Introduction

You've heard it many times; perhaps you've even said it yourself: "What this country needs is a really great leader like George Washington or Abraham Lincoln—someone with real integrity and vision who can bring us together and get us back on the right track!"

I hear that lament frequently, and sometimes I'm even one of the people who give voice to it. But deep down I wonder how much truth lies behind this fine sentiment. If we are to raise up great leaders for our own age, we probably don't want to clone the leaders of the past. Washington was an extraordinary leader for the extraordinary times in which he lived, but he probably wouldn't be a particularly effective president or military leader today.

Washington and Lincoln are both personal heroes of mine, and this book will provide some perspective on what helped make them great. But one of the most important and contrarian points we can make about leadership is that it is highly situational and contingent; the leader who succeeds in one context at one point in time won't necessarily succeed in a different context at the same time, or in the same context at a different time.

The very concept of leadership is elusive and tricky. It's hard to define in a way that is satisfactory to everyone, although most people believe they know it when they see it. Certainly there are natural leaders who seem to gravitate effortlessly to positions of power and authority. And yet many of the world's greatest leaders demonstrated relatively little aptitude for leadership in their youth, but instead learned this esoteric art through study, apprenticeship and practice.

Of all the different kinds of human capital, leadership may well be the most rare and precious. Think of the companies one can point to that were going down the tubes in spite of gaggles of consultants and new plans and policies, until finally the CEO was booted out, a new leader was brought in, and the company turned around as though by magic. History abounds with similar examples among armies, universities, churches, and nations.

But there is also the other kind of leadership transition, in which the untimely loss of a talented and effective leader proves disastrous for the organization he was leading. Try as they may, a succession of new leaders simply cannot stem the inexorable decline of the very same organization which a few months or years before was at the peak of health and vitality.

Moreover, sometimes whole societies lose their ability to produce great leaders. As Americans, we tend to believe that the larger society of which we are a part is steadily improving with each passing decade. But the fact is, the twentieth century was far more barbaric than the preceding four centuries, and as such represented a severe backsliding in terms of man's inhumanity to man. Part of this backsliding was attributable to a dramatic improvement in the technologies of death and coercion, but much of it was the result of our inability to produce leaders who could persuasively articulate a humane moral philosophy in an age dominated by technological change.

There are numerous cases of societies which lost their earlier highly developed culture, and retrogressed to a more primitive way of life. In some of these cases external factors, such as invasion or drought, clearly played a role, but in many cases it would seem that the retrogression was due to a failure of will and a lack of leadership.

So if leadership is largely situational and contingent, why read books on leadership at all? Why shouldn't a person simply jump into a leadership role and sink or swim on her own merits? Granted, there is no infallible step-by-step formula for becoming an effective leader. But leadership *can* be taught and learned. More explicitly, a person can develop her own potential for leadership by reading about what's worked for others and then selectively applying those lessons to her own situation.

The purpose of this book is to get you to think about leaders and leadership from a fresh and original point of view—from what I like to call a contrarian perspective. By contrarian I don't mean counter to all conventional wisdom—indeed, much of the conventional wisdom about leadership (and about most other things for that matter) is absolutely true. But just as you can't become an effective leader by trying to mimic a famous leader from the past, so you can't develop your full leadership potential, or even fully appreciate the art of leadership, by slavishly adhering to conventional wisdom. The key is to break free, if only fleetingly, from the bonds of conventional thinking so as to bring your natural creativity and intellectual independence to the fore.

Many of the concepts expressed in this book will seem strange and counterintuitive at first: think gray, see double, never completely trust an expert, read what your competition doesn't read, never make a decision yourself that can reasonably be delegated to a subordinate, ignore sunk costs, work for those who work for you, know which hill you're willing to die on, shoot your own horse, sometimes allow the led to lead the leader, and know the difference between being leader and doing leader. Do all these concepts run completely counter to conventional wisdom? No. But they certainly challenge conventional thinking in ways I believe you'll find both stimulating and beneficial.

I've based this book on my twenty-seven years of experience as a senior leader at three major research universities, including nine years as president of the State University of New York at

Buffalo and ten years as president of the University of Southern California. I've also served over the years on fourteen corporate boards in a wide variety of industries, which has allowed me to observe and interact closely with scores of business leaders. Then too, as a university president I've had a chance to work with hundreds of political leaders and government officials both here and abroad, and with numerous leaders of synagogues and churches, labor unions, eleemosynary organizations and cultural institutions.

Finally, I've had the rare privilege of working with over two hundred of USC's brightest and most ambitious young leaders through a course I've taught each spring semester over the past six years with my friend and colleague Warren Bennis, who is one of the world's most noted experts on leadership. This course, entitled "The Art and Adventure of Leadership," draws students from departments and schools across the university. Each year we select 40 outstanding juniors and seniors out of a pool of more than 160 who apply. In seminar settings, in small groups, and through individual study, these students examine the lives and careers of twenty historical and contemporary leaders, from King David to Washington to Napoleon to Gandhi to Martin Luther King to Margaret Thatcher. They read over one thousand pages of text, interact with nearly a dozen guest speakers representing a variety of leadership roles, write a dozen four-page papers, and complete a major group project.

Even though my professorship is in electrical engineering, teaching this course has been one of the most satisfying academic experiences of my career. The no-holds-barred discussions we have had with our students about leaders and leadership have given both Warren and me numerous new insights into this fascinating and important area of human behavior.

This book is divided into chapters which can, for the most part, be read out of sequence. The good news is that it has no pretensions of being an all-of-a-piece philosophical treatise which requires the reader to buy the whole thing or nothing at all. On the contrary, feel free to keep what appeals to you and simply forget the rest.

You'll find that each contrarian point in the text is illustrated with examples both ancient and modern from politics, business, the military, religion and academe. The book ends with a case study of contrarian leadership at USC which synthesizes many of the points made in earlier chapters.

The art of leadership, as well as individual practitioners of that art, are always works in progress. They are never finished and complete; rather, they are always evolving, always changing, never static. Let me invite you to participate in this process of artistic evolution, and to do so from a contrarian point of view. If this book provides you with fresh insight about this most noble and necessary art, it will have served its purpose well.

Chapter 1

Thinking Gray, and Free

Contrarian leaders think differently from the people around them. In particular, such leaders are able to maintain their intellectual independence by thinking gray, and enhance their intellectual creativity by thinking free.

Conventional wisdom considers it a valuable skill to be able to make judgments as quickly as possible, and conventional wisdom may well be right when it comes to managers. But contrarian wisdom argues that, for leaders, judgments as to the truth or falsity of information or the merits of new ideas should be arrived at as slowly and subtly as possible—and in many cases not at all.

One of the most rewarding aspects of teaching a class on leadership has been the opportunity to watch bright undergraduates learn to "think gray" while holding firmly to their core principles. Thinking gray is an extraordinarily uncommon characteristic which requires a good deal of effort to develop. But it is one of the most important skills which a leader can acquire.

Most people are binary and instant in their judgments; that is, they immediately categorize things as good or bad, true or false, black or white, friend or foe. A truly effective leader, however, needs to be able to see the shades of gray inherent in a situation in order to make wise decisions as to how to proceed.

The essence of thinking gray is this: don't form an opinion about an important matter until you've heard all the relevant facts and arguments, or until circumstances force you to form an opin-ion without recourse to all the facts (which happens occasionally, but much less frequently than one might imagine). F. Scott Fitz-gerald once described something similar to thinking gray when he observed that the test of a first-rate mind is the ability to hold two opposing thoughts at the same time while still retaining the abil-ity to function.

Generally the only time the average person is instructed to think gray is when he is called to serve on a jury in a court of law (which may be one reason so many people regard jury duty as a colossal pain). A juror is expected to suspend judgment until he has heard all the facts and arguments, and then and only then is he asked to reach a conclusion. I've never served on a jury myself, but talking with people who have and observing juries up close have convinced me that most jurors begin to make up their minds about a case before the trial even begins. And I suspect that most judges do as well.

After all, thinking gray is not a natural act, especially for peo-ple who see themselves as leaders. Our typical view of great lead-ers is that they are bold and decisive people who are strongly governed by their passions and prejudices. Who could imagine a Teddy Roosevelt or a Vince Lombardi thinking gray?

A black-and-white binary approach to thinking may in fact be a successful strategy for some leaders, especially if they must deal daily with fight-or-flight situations. But even many of the world's most noted military leaders were adroit at thinking gray on the battlefield. Napoleon, Washington, and Rommel all knew the value of suspending judgment about important matters, and especially about the validity of incoming intelligence, until the last possible moment.

I recall once chatting with a friend who told me about some-thing she had just heard on the television news. I responded, "That's really interesting."

She looked a little hurt. "You don't believe me, do you?"

I said, surprised, "What do you mean, I don't believe you?"

She said, "You don't believe what I just told you."

I said, "I believe you're telling me exactly what you heard on television."

"But you don't believe it."

"I don't *disbelieve* it."

"Steve," she asked, "how can you do that? How can you sit there and hear something that was said on TV and not believe it or disbelieve it?"

And I replied, "Because there's no need for me to decide right now whether what the newscaster said is true or false. In fact, I'll probably never have to reach a conclusion on this matter at all, which I regard as a great blessing!"

The person with whom I was speaking is a very intelligent and well-educated woman. But like most people, and unfortunately like so many would-be leaders, she feels an obligation to immediately classify everything she reads or hears as either true or false, good or bad, right or wrong, useful or useless.

For the vast majority of people, giving in to this natural compulsion toward binary thinking is relatively harmless. But for leaders it can lead to disaster.

There are three very real dangers to effective leadership associated with binary thinking. One is that the leader forms opinions before it is necessary to do so, and in the process closes his mind to facts and arguments that may subsequently come to his attention. The second danger is flip-flopping. A leader hears something in favor of a proposition and decides on the spot that the proposition must be true. Later that same day he hears an argument against the proposition and decides that the proposition must be false. Many failed leaders have tended to believe the last thing they heard from the last person they talked to, thereby putting themselves and their followers through mental (and sometime physical) contortions which were both unnecessary and counterproductive.

The third danger relates to an observation by the German philosopher Friedrich Nietzsche, to the effect that people tend to believe that which they sense is strongly believed by others. A well-developed ability to think gray is the best defense a leader can have against this kind of assault on his intellectual independence. Leaders may want to nurture a herd mentality among their followers, but they should never succumb to such thinking themselves.

Nietzsche's point was beautifully illustrated by an experiment fashioned by psychologist Solomon Asch a half-century ago and repeated by others many times since then. In the experiment, eight subjects, supposedly chosen at random, were brought together in a room and shown a series of cards on which were printed four vertical lines. Each subject was asked in turn to identify which one of the three lines on the right side of the card was the same length as the line on the left side of the card. The experiment was arranged so that seven of the eight "subjects" were in fact ringers who, with conviction and sincerity, would each identify the same one of the right-hand lines as being equal in length to the left-hand line, when in fact it was not. The one true subject in this experiment was then faced with either going along with the judgment of the group and declaring as true something he knew to be false, or taking a position which was at odds with the consensus opinion of his peers. Roughly *three-quarters* of the subjects went against their better judgment and joined in with the false consensus at least once.

As in so many other areas that are essential to effective leadership, the popular media are a major stumbling block to thinking gray. There is no such thing as an unbiased article in a newspaper or an objective sound bite on television news. On the contrary, reporters and editors are trained experts at getting you to believe what it is they have to say and to adopt their point of view. Indeed, à la Nietzsche, the media want you to believe that everyone else (or at least, every other *important* person) believes what it is they have to say. It is precisely this patina of believability and respectability that makes the popular media so attractive to us, especially when their messages comport with our own passions and prejudices. And it is precisely this same patina that stands in the way of our thinking gray.

The binary point of view already inherent in the popular media has become more pronounced, as straight coverage of politics has moved into a sports-section-like obsession with identifying winners and losers and successes and failures. A horse-race approach to political coverage, however, can rarely address adequately the complexities and nuances of developments in public policy.

Lest we go too far with this idea, let it be said that thinking gray—suspending our binary instincts—is really necessary for a leader for only the weightiest of issues. If he were to attempt to think gray about everything, his brain would become a jumbled mess. Decisions about clothes, food, popular music, and so forth are usually made in an off-the-cuff binary way, and that's perfectly fine.

However, these ordinary and routine types of decisions offer a wonderful chance to develop the discipline of thinking gray. One can use these situations as opportunities to practice suspending judgment. You don't have to decide right away whether you like a person you've just met, or whether you might eventually be able to appreciate a new food you've just tried, or whether you should see a particular movie you've recently heard about. Just for fun (or for practice) you can file away your first impressions about these and other relatively trivial matters, and reach conclusions with respect to them at a later date (or not at all). A great benefit of this exercise is that, when a truly important leadership issue surfaces, you will have had some practice in thinking gray.

Aristotle noted that, when carpenters wish to straighten a warped board, they don't put it in a jig that simply holds it straight; rather they put it in a jig that bends it in the opposite direction from that in which it is warped. After a week or two in this reverse-bending configuration, the board naturally springs back to a straight shape when it is released from the jig. So it is when we attempt to correct our own weaknesses. We must bend over backward in an effort to overcompensate, and in that way we just might achieve a reasonable middle ground. Forcing ourselves to bend over backward by thinking gray with respect to a few everyday matters is an excellent way to overcome our natural inclination to think in black and white.

Thinking gray is decidedly *not* the same thing as thinking skeptically. The skeptic initially places everything he hears or reads in the "not true" box, with an implied willingness to move things to the "true" box if the accumulated evidence warrants such a transfer. There's often a hint of cynicism about the skeptic that can be very off-putting to followers. It's difficult for people to be inspired by a Doubting Thomas.

By contrast, the contrarian leader who can think gray doesn't place things he hears or reads in either the "not true" or the "true" box. He is as open to enthusiastically embracing a new idea as he is to rejecting it. And he can truthfully compliment a lieutenant for having come up with a new idea or observation, without misleading the lieutenant as to whether he (the leader) believes it to be good or true or useful.

A close cousin of thinking gray is what I like to call thinking free—free, that is, from all prior restraints. It's popular these days to talk about "thinking out of the box" or "brainstorming," but thinking free takes that process of inventiveness to the next level.

The difference between thinking out of the box and thinking free can be understood when we imagine ourselves coming out of a heated swimming pool on a cool, brisk day. When we merely think out of the box, we stay in the cold just long enough to feel slightly uncomfortable, and then hastily retreat either back into the warm pool or indoors. But when we are truly thinking free, we stay out in the cold until we shiver and our teeth chatter. It's the ability to tolerate the cold long after it becomes unpleasant—to forcibly sustain our thinking free for more than a fleeting moment—that leads to the greatest innovations.

The key to thinking free is first to allow your mind to contemplate really outrageous ideas, and only subsequently apply the constraints of practicality, practicability, legality, cost, time, and ethics. As with thinking gray, thinking free is an unnatural act; not one person in a thousand can do it without enormous effort.

Here's a simple example. A leader brings a group of people together who share a common goal (e.g., keeping their company afloat in a brutally competitive market), but who have widely varying opinions as to how the goal might best be achieved. The leader asks each person in turn to propose an off-the-wall idea for achieving the goal, with the proviso that every other person in the group must respond with at least two reasons why the idea will work. The result is often surliness or sullen silence on the part of the participants. Most people are simply unable to force themselves to think positively for even a few minutes about an idea which they believe in their hearts is stupid, wrongheaded, immoral, impractical, or illegal.

Now please do not misunderstand me; I am not suggesting that leaders should pursue evil or illegal or ridiculous ideas. On the contrary, I have found that one's principles, passions and prejudices always reassert control after a few minutes of thinking free. But during those few minutes the leader or his or her associates just might come up with a truly original idea.

Congenital naysayers are among the greatest stumbling blocks to thinking free. Rather than imagining how a new idea might possibly work, they instinctively think of all the reasons why it won't. They sincerely believe they're doing everyone a favor by reducing the amount of time spent on bad or foolish ideas. But what they really do is undermine the creativity that can be harvested from thinking free.

Most new inventions are merely novel combinations of devices or techniques that already exist. Thus, the key to successful invention often lies in getting one's brain to imagine new combinations of existing elements that solve a problem in a way no one has ever thought of before.

My favorite way to stimulate this kind of thinking free is to force myself to contemplate absolutely outrageous and impossible ways to address a particular problem. For example, in 1967 I was struggling to invent a new way to control a dishwasher, in order to replace the ubiquitous (and troublesome) clock-motor timer. At one point I lay on the floor and forced myself to imagine hay bales, elephants, planets, ladybugs, sofas, microbes, newspapers, hydroelectric dams, French horns, electrons and trees, each in turn and in various combinations controlling a dishwasher.

This exercise was, to say the least, extremely difficult and disconcerting, so much so that I could only do it for ten minutes at a time. But after a few such sessions I suddenly saw in my mind's eye an almost complete circuit diagram for a digital electronic control system for a home appliance. This system was unlike anything I or others had ever contemplated before. As a consequence my colleagues and I were able to establish a very strong patent position in this particular area of technology, and my invention was eventually employed in hundreds of millions of home appliances around the world.

As improbable as it might sound, this same approach to thinking free can lead to novel ways of addressing some of the competitive, political, legal, policy and bureaucratic challenges one must confront as a leader. The key is to break free for just a few minutes from the incredibly tight constraints that rule our thinking almost all of the time, even when we dream or engage in so-called free association.

Really thinking free is hard work, and it usually requires a good deal of effort and determination beyond simple daydreaming or mental freewheeling. It's tough to break out of the deep ruts in which our minds normally run. But the benefits that accrue to the leader from thinking free can be truly spectacular.

Of course, microbes, hay bales and elephants never found their way into my application for a patent on a new way to control a home appliance. On the contrary, the solution to this problem involved a simple combination of standard electronic components—so simple, so nearly obvious, that I wondered why no one had ever thought of it before.

That's the way it is with so many innovations—they seem obvious once they've been discovered and deployed. But prior to that time, they are anything but obvious. For example, the benefits of universal adult suffrage seem obvious to twenty-first century Americans, but it took millennia after the development of writing to discover and implement this novel idea (which was not fully adopted in England until 1928, when women were finally given the vote). The wheel-and-axle seems an obvious bit of technology to us today, but it was not discovered until thousands of years after the invention of the roller, and many human societies *never* discovered the wheel-and-axle on their own. The auto mall would appear to be an obvious way to increase the sales of new cars, but when I was a boy the Ford dealer in town wanted to be located as far away as possible from the Chevrolet dealer.

It's well known among engineers that the most important inventions in a particular field are often made by people who are new to that field—people who are too naïve and ignorant to know all the reasons why something can't be done, and who are therefore able to think more freely about seemingly intractable problems. The same is true of the leadership of institutions: it's often fresh blood and a fresh perspective from the outside that can turn an ailing organization around.

When my wife and I were interviewing in the early 1980s for the presidency of the State University of New York at Buffalo (SUNY-Buffalo, or the University at Buffalo, or UB for short), we saw a university with great underlying strengths and numerous superficial problems. Unfortunately, the problematic surface was all that was perceived by most of UB's constituencies at the time.

Never in our lives had we encountered a university that was so down on itself or that was held in such low esteem by so many of its own faculty, students, administrators, townspeople, and alumni. The body politic of the university seemed to be bruised all over—whenever we touched it, no matter how gently, it seemed to quiver and shrink back a bit.

For example, during the four months prior to my officially assuming the presidency in March of 1982, and during my first few months in office, I spoke directly with hundreds of UB's constituents. Almost invariably these conversations began with the other person saying something negative about the university. And during this same period I never met a single student who said that he or she was *proud* to be attending UB.

However, from my wife's and my perspective, the inner core, the infrastructure if you will, of the University at Buffalo was in exceedingly good health. We saw a university which had an excellent (albeit somewhat dispirited) faculty, competitive faculty salaries, good students who were willing to work hard, a loyal and supportive governing council, competent and dedicated staff, an active university foundation, a brand-new physical plant, mostly new scientific equipment, an outstanding library, and a long and distinguished academic history.

We also recognized that UB was in fact SUNY's flagship campus, although the vast majority of New Yorkers, and indeed most Buffalonians, would not have agreed with that statement in 1982. It seemed clear to us that, as the flagship public institution in a large and prosperous state, UB had a shot at becoming one of America's premier public universities.

There were of course formidable obstacles blocking UB's development. In addition to the spiritual malaise cited earlier, there loomed the fact that the city of Buffalo and its environs were mired in a deep recession, with unemployment rates running as high as 15 percent. Then too, the entire SUNY system was caught in the suffocating embrace of a huge state bureaucracy which was trying its best to micromanage everything at the university from coffee cups to student-contact hours.

And finally there was the fact that most New Yorkers seemed to view public higher education as being inherently inferior to private higher education. I recall how shocked I was when, early in my tenure at UB, I heard a trustee of the SUNY system say in public that "SUNY is the college of last resort." Good grief! I should have thought that every trustee would see the SUNY system as the college of *first* resort for *all* classes of New Yorkers, as is the case with the great public universities in other states.

Nonetheless, in spite of these difficulties and problems, my wife and I were convinced that UB's future was potentially very bright. Fortunately most members of the UB Council and a significant number of faculty and staff agreed.

The next nine years more than justified Kathryn's and my seemingly unfounded optimism. By the end of that period UB had been elected to the prestigious Association of American Universities (only 61 of the more than 3,500 colleges and universities in America are members of the AAU; UB was the first public university in New York or New England to have been elected), sponsored research funding had tripled, applications for admission had doubled, we had completed or begun construction of more than two million square feet of new buildings at a cost of more than $400 million, UB was raising more private funds each year than all the other SUNY campuses combined, and *U.S. News and World Report* had named UB as one of the five most rapidly rising universities in the country.

Was it a miracle? No. Was the president a genius? No. It was just that my wife and I, coming from our experiences at the University of Nebraska, Purdue University and the University of Illinois, were able to see UB and its surrounding community from a very different perspective. In other words, our thinking about UB was freer and less constrained than that of our colleagues and peers in western New York.

We often speak of the need for leaders to have vision. Creative imagination, which relates to the ability to think free, may in the end be every bit as important as vision.

Many of us were tested on spatial relations in school, being asked to look at a number of pieces of a puzzle and imagine different ways in which those pieces might be combined. A similar act of imagination is a powerful tool for leaders.

The leader has to be able to imagine different organizational combinations in his mind and see how they will play out. He has to be able to move people around in his mind and grasp how they would respond to new situations. He has to be able to move resources and budgets around and be able to discern how those moves would affect the bottom line. He needs to be able to look at complex human situations and sense how the outcome would be affected depending on the sequence in which he interacts with various participants.

If he cannot do these things effectively using only his imagination—if he can only work with tangible, concrete data—he may well fail as a leader. It is far too time-consuming, far too risky and far too expensive to conduct an actual experiment to test the feasibility of every new idea. Generally speaking, a leader must be able to accurately play out contingencies within the arena of his imagination.

But here's a bit of good news for would-be leaders who find it difficult to think free, and whose imaginations are, shall we say, a bit underdeveloped. It's not absolutely necessary that a leader himself, in order to be effective, be a creative genius overflowing with original and inventive ideas. In many cases it's sufficient if the leader simply recognizes and nurtures thinking free among his followers, and then capitalizes on *their* creative ideas and imaginations. Indeed, many successful leaders would say it's more important that a leader's lieutenants be able to think free than it is for the leader himself to do so. (J. Robert Oppenheimer once said of his Manhattan Project team, "What we don't know we explain to each other.") Realistically, though, a leader whose own mind is stuck in a rut will find it very difficult to value imaginative thinking on the part of those around him.

One must always keep in mind that leadership is an art, not a science. Effective management may be a science (although I have my doubts), but effective leadership is purely an art. In this sense, leadership is more akin to music, painting and poetry than it is to more routinized endeavors. When Franklin Roosevelt met Orson Welles, the president showed great deference to the media pioneer and actor, saying he wished he were as gifted a performing artist as Welles—to which Welles replied, "With all due respect, Mr. President, you are!"

All of the arts, when practiced at the highest levels of excellence, depend on a steady stream of fresh ideas and creative imagination. Make no mistake, Mozart was thinking free when he composed, even though his music may sound canonical today. As a former professional musician, I know that the best solos in jazz occur when the soloist frees his mind of prior constraints and makes up entirely new musical associations as he goes along. Can anyone view Picasso's paintings or Frank Gehry's buildings and not see flashes of unrestrained thought and imagination? And when I read Shakespeare I hear the cacophonous undertones of thinking free—his constant testing of unusual juxtapositions of words, his novel metaphors and similes, his making up of new words and stretching the meanings of old ones with impunity.

So it is with effective leadership. The leader whose thinking is constrained within well-worn ruts, who is completely governed by his established passions and prejudices, who is incapable of thinking either gray or free, and who can't even appropriate the creative imagination and fresh ideas of those around him, is as anachronistic and ineffective as the dinosaur. He may by dint of circumstances remain in power, but his followers would almost certainly be better off without him.

Chapter 2

Artful Listening

The average person suffers from three delusions: (1) that he is a good driver, (2) that he has a good sense of humor, and (3) that he is a good listener. Most people, however, including many leaders, are terrible listeners; they actually think talking is more important than listening. But contrarian leaders know it is better to listen first and talk later. And when they listen, they do so artfully.

A contrarian leader is an artful listener, not because it makes people feel good (which it does), but rather because artful listening is an excellent means of acquiring new ideas and gathering and assessing information.

If a leader can listen attentively without rushing to judgment, he will often get a fresh perspective that will help him think independently. This kind of leader listens carefully to his official advisers, especially those in his inner circle; he occasionally listens to self-appointed advisers—even the most obnoxious among them; and he continues to listen to his inner voice which reflects his own personal experience and creative impulses.

"Minds are of three kinds," Machiavelli wrote. "One is capable of thinking for itself; another is able to understand the thinking of others; and a third can neither think for itself nor understand the thinking of others. The first is of the highest excellence, the second is excellent, and the third is worthless." While Machiavelli makes great sense here, I would alter his words to say that the best mind of all for a leader is one that can both think for itself *and* understand the thinking of others. The latter ability depends on artful listening.

Artful listening is important for maintaining the contrarian leader's intellectual independence. It enables him to see things through the eyes of his followers while at the same time seeing things from his own unique perspective—a process which I like to call "seeing double." The contrarian leader prizes and cultivates his ability to simultaneously view things from two or more perspectives. He can listen to what others have to say about important issues without surrendering his principles or his creative judgment. He avoids becoming immobilized by conflicting points of view, and he never abdicates to others the responsibility for fashioning his own unique vision.

A leader's inner circle of advisers should be founded on mutual understanding and trust. It should be comprised entirely of individuals who are committed to the institution's and the leader's best interests, and whose filters, prejudices and attitudes are well understood by the leader. Toward that end it is usually best to keep one's inner circle of advisers relatively small—typically no more than eight.

At USC the five senior vice presidents who report directly to me, along with my wife, comprise the core of my inner circle of advisers. Each of these persons is free to say, and willing to say, "Steve, your proposed approach to this situation is just plain wrong!" We frequently have no-holds-barred discussions among two or more of us. But all of the senior vice presidents understand that once a decision has been made, we will carry out that decision as a team.

My closest and longest-term adviser is my wife of forty years, Kathryn Sample. I trust her more than any other person, and I take harsher criticism from her than from anyone else, because I believe she always has my best interests at heart. Kathryn certainly knows my strengths and weaknesses more intimately than other people. Moreover, after four decades of our living together, her personal agenda is essentially congruent with mine (although our *perspectives* are radically different). Of course I don't always follow my wife's advice, any more than I do that of any other adviser, but I always listen to her opinions with great care and interest. It's a plus in our relationship that Kathryn has no desire whatsoever to share in the authority of the presidency or be the de facto deputy president.

One should never underestimate the value of a stable long-term marriage to the success of a leader. In his classic book *On Becoming a Leader*, Warren Bennis notes that the overwhelming majority of successful corporate CEOs and other leaders whom he interviewed were involved in very stable long-term marriages, and that these leaders felt their spouses were major factors in their success. Many people have the impression these days that a person can scarcely be a successful politician, military leader, corporate CEO or university president unless he has been involved in myriad affairs and changed spouses at regular intervals. But the facts bespeak otherwise.

A leader's inner circle of advisers carries a special importance as the only group with whom he consults on the full, broad array of matters within his purview. Machiavelli argues in *The Prince* that the inner circle should consist of "the wise men of the state" who are instructed to speak honestly and candidly on any matters on which the prince seeks their counsel, and he goes on to say that the prince should seek their counsel on every matter of importance.

Harry Truman very deliberately sought out advisers, such as George C. Marshall and Dean Acheson, who knew more or were wiser than he. That takes considerable courage and humility on the part of the leader, more than most can summon. (In Chapter 8, "Work for Those Who Work for You," we'll discuss the effect of such an approach in recruiting lieutenants.)

Machiavelli saw the inner circle of advisers as a means whereby the prince could safeguard himself against flatterers, who prey upon every leader's natural desire to think well of himself.

Machiavelli's approach continues to have value. It's not easy to accept unpleasant advice and even personal criticism from one's closest advisers. Yet Machiavelli insisted that a leader should demand this degree of candor from his inner circle, and should show indignation if he senses he isn't getting it.

Granted, it is as difficult for an adviser to send harsh messages to his boss as it is to receive them. After all, advisers have their own personal agendas; they therefore have a natural tendency to choose their battles, especially if they function not only as sounding boards but also as line operating officers. "Does the president really want me to be candid here?" an adviser might wonder. "I'm going to need her support later on when we get to my item on the agenda, so why should I upset her now over this item in which I have no real stake?"

Many leaders reject the idea of using line officers as inner-circle advisers because such people inevitably have a narrower set of priorities and perspectives than the leader. "Charlie is responsible only for manufacturing, not for sales, engineering, marketing or finance. How can he possibly advise me (the leader) on issues affecting the whole company?" Leaders who feel this way generally choose their inner circle of advisers from among staff, as opposed to line, personnel. But as we shall see later on, staff people bring with them their own special problems and limitations.

Personally, I prefer line officers as inner-circle advisers (my wife being the exception) because they know what it's like to take the heat for their decisions—how painful it is to be the person who has to let people go or close down a program or reallocate resources.

But whether staff or line, advisers are human beings, not machines. It is to be expected that they will have their own agendas. Every person, when he opines, has an agenda, perhaps so well hidden that he may not recognize it himself. That's why I expect my inner-circle of advisers to have openly acknowledged agendas.

It helps us work together to see whether and how their individual priorities can be integrated into an overall plan.

Far too often an ambitious adviser will prostitute his special access to the leader to get his own agenda implemented while hiding behind the leader's skirts. This is a great temptation for an adviser: to use the leader's power in order to hurt a rival or carry out a plan without reprisal or accountability if the tactic fails. Trust within the inner circle is the best antidote for this disease.

Leaders must remember that creating genuine trust is not like dumping instant coffee into hot water. A leader who seeks to operate effectively over the long term needs to minimize turnover among his senior advisers in order to allow trust and candor to develop on a solid foundation.

On the other hand, every organization, large or small, has a *curia* of sorts, a top level of bureaucracy analogous to those persons in the Vatican closest to the pope. A curia can easily become incestuous, with each person voicing and revoicing the perspective of his fellow curiales. An inner circle that becomes too narrow and ingrown is a significant stumbling block to effective leadership.

Boards of directors, trustees and regents, employee committees, unions, faculty senates, vestries, elders, presidential commissions, task forces, Boy Scout councils—all of these bodies fall into the category of elected and appointed advisers. In the case of boards of directors and boards of trustees, these "advisers" have in fact the authority to approve or reject the leader's plans and ultimately the power to hire and fire the leader himself. But unless there is a revolution afoot, even these governing bodies usually operate as advisers to the leader.

Several years ago I made a presentation to the Finance Committee of the USC Board of Trustees about a project in which I was particularly interested, and for which I needed the committee's approval. At the end of my presentation, one of our smartest, toughest, and most influential trustees said, "You know, Steve, that has to be the dumbest plan I've ever heard of. It's inconceivable to me that your plan would work under any circumstances. But hey, Steve, you're the president, and if you want to give this plan a try, I'll back you 100 percent!" After thinking it over for a millisecond or two I had the good sense to say, "Thanks, Bill, for your support, but if you don't mind, I'd like to pull this plan from today's agenda and give it a little more thought." In this case my governing board was serving as an official adviser to me, not as my boss, and I was artfully listening to their advice.

When it comes to elected and appointed advisory groups (and self-appointed advisers as well), the main challenge for the leader is figuring out whom they really represent and for whom they can credibly speak. We have 2,500 full-time faculty members at USC, each of whom enjoys enormous professional independence. Does anyone really believe that on a given Wednesday afternoon a faculty senate of forty-three members can discern and articulate the collective thinking of USC's faculty as a whole? Of course not. But because its members are elected by the faculty as a whole, the faculty senate can in fact represent the interests of their peers in important ways.

Perhaps we might usefully paraphrase the philosopher Eric Hoffer here, to the effect that a leader should listen very carefully to his elected and appointed advisers but never take them *too* seriously. In particular, the leader should never attach more importance to the words of an official adviser than the adviser's true status among his constituents would warrant.

Unsolicited advice confronts a leader at every turn—and this is especially true for a university president. Letters, faxes, e-mails and phone calls come in to my office; an alumnus bumps into me at the grocery store; a professor corners me at the faculty club; a student organization sends me its latest manifesto for improving the university. Machiavelli suggests that it's a waste of time to listen to such advice at all. I disagree. Unsolicited advice often provides the leader with an opportunity to learn something he'd never learn from his official advisers. At the same time, however, such advice can be grossly misleading.

Often a leader will be approached by individuals purporting to represent others. In some cases these people are legitimate representatives of a particular constituency; at other times they are self-appointed. In either case the leader must always keep in mind that the most dedicated and vocal members of any constituency may not represent the collective thinking of that group at all.

For example, if you hold an elective office, how might you discern on any given day what the voters in your district are thinking? How would you measure how firmly they hold their convictions? Would you weigh the letters or count the e-mails on one side or the other of an issue? Would you take a poll?

In physics there is a well-established law known as the Heisenberg Uncertainty Principle. It says, in essence, that under certain circumstances the very process of measurement can affect the outcome of a measurement in unpredictable ways. We can see a similar uncertainty principle at work when it comes to judging the mood of voters or customers or faculty—the very act of asking the question can dramatically skew the answer.

The academic landscape is littered with the corpses of deposed deans whose faculties were reasonably content until some small group of professors decided to take a poll on the question: "Should Dean Higgens be asked to step down in view of the problems currently confronting our college?" And lo and behold, it turned out a majority of the faculty agreed it was time to cashier old Higgens, even though *prior* to the poll most of them couldn't have cared less about Dean Higgens one way or the other.

Be wary when an adviser, be he official or self-appointed, tells you that "our customers want this" or "our employees want that" or "the faculty are upset about such and such." The contrarian leader never takes such counsel at face value; the first question she asks is, "*Who* is saying what to *whom*?" One needs to understand

Example

whether the person giving the advice is communicating opinions from two people or two hundred and whether he heard those opinions directly or indirectly.

Often an adviser hears a few people say things that comport with his own agenda. Then, subconsciously or otherwise, he exaggerates in his own mind the support for that agenda among the larger body politic. At other times the reporting process is simply sloppy, with secondhand comments and rumors being passed along as hard facts. At such times the leader must be extremely artful as she sorts through a mishmash of contradictory advice. Occasionally she must simply stop listening to anything other than her own inner voice.

The person who can turn listening into an art is one who goes beyond merely listening passively; he becomes intensely interested in what's being said and draws out the other person. In the process he gains not only additional details, but also valuable information about the filters and biases of the person presenting the information. Active listening, with relevant and probing questions, can help the leader find out if the speaker is being slipshod or meticulous in his reporting, and can create an atmosphere of accountability in which the speaker realizes he is expected to offer defensible information rather than mere pontification.

There is much to be learned from listening to two different people separately recount the same event. No matter how hard he tries, a single human being can never give you a completely unbiased report on any event or issue; he will always give you a view that is filtered to some extent through his own prejudices. However, if you make it a point to get independent assessments of the same event from two or more people whose biases you know, you'll be in a better position to discern the truth of the matter. If I know that one of my senior vice presidents tends to take a cynical view of most events and another tends to take an overly optimistic view, it is often fruitful for me to sit down with each of them separately and carefully listen to their individual accounts of a particular situation.

The conventional rules of social discourse which most leaders learn on their way to the top do not generally equip them to be artful listeners. For one thing, leaders who listen attentively and carefully run the risk of being misunderstood. In particular, sympathetic listening by a leader can be misinterpreted by his followers as giving his assent. Franklin Roosevelt suffered especially from this problem. Almost everyone who had a private conversation with FDR left feeling the president agreed with him, while in fact Roosevelt might well have been in total disagreement with the person doing the speaking. This shortcoming on Roosevelt's part led to a lot of hard feelings and battles royal within his administration.

Thus it is the *leader's* responsibility to ensure that the person who is speaking to him is not inadvertently misled by the leader's genuine efforts to understand and appreciate what's being said. Achieving this delicate balance is a fine art.

In Chapter 1 we discussed the value of thinking gray—taking in information and suspending judgment with respect to its truth or falsity as long as possible. An important part of thinking gray for a leader is *listening* gray—absorbing stories, reports, complaints, posturings, accusations, extravagant claims, and prejudices without immediately offering a definitive response.

Moreover, the leader is in a position to hear things differently from how they're heard by followers closer to the front lines, who may feel compelled to protect their staff or their own policies. Because the leader is often more detached from a situation, he has a chance to rise above defensiveness and acknowledge concerns without making judgments.

Occasionally someone approaches me to complain—in person, or by letter, fax or e-mail—about an experience or interaction he had with some of our staff or students that left him angry or dissatisfied. My first reaction is to acknowledge his concerns by offering what I call a "temporizing response." I might quickly send a letter saying, "Mr. Smith, the kind of behavior you described in your recent letter to me is totally unacceptable here at USC. I have asked Senior Vice President Jones to look into the matter; she will report her findings and actions directly to you and to me within ten days." What I *don't* say is, "Mr. Smith, what happened to you is terrible," because I do not in fact *know* what happened to him, and I won't be in a position to form a judgment on that question until the other side (or sides) of the story have been heard.

The discipline here is to not be dismissive or unresponsive on the one hand, or rush to judgment on the other. Mr. Smith complained to the president, and he received a prompt reply from the president. My reply was sympathetic and indicated that his values and mine were in close harmony. In this way Mr. Smith knows that we're listening to him, and that we are willing to change our ways in response to his complaint if changes are in order. But my response also made it clear that I was not necessarily accepting his rendition of what happened.

In fact I may never have to reach a conclusion as to what actually happened—it's usually a matter for someone else to decide. After I assure the complaining party that I've taken notice of his concerns, I send a note to the appropriate senior officer asking her to look into it. I don't send her a searing message telling her to fix the problem; I simply say something like, "Mr. Smith claims to have been mistreated by some of our students. I have no idea if his claims are true, but if they are, please tell me what *you* are going to do about it."

A related point is that I always refer the matter to a senior vice president who reports directly to me—not to the manager who is closest to the problem. By holding the senior officer accountable for fixing the problem, all the staff under her are also accountable. If I were to directly charge a middle manager with correcting a problem, I would be undercutting the senior vice president's authority and responsibility for that problem. Moreover, in a short period of time that middle manager would feel he was reporting to me, and not to the cognizant senior vice president.

There is one airline I use more than any other. Occasionally I'll write the CEO of that airline a letter complimenting one of his staff for exceptional service, and occasionally I send him a letter of complaint. I've always been amused by the fact that he responds personally to complimentary letters, but the responses I receive to complaints always come from a staff assistant. What a wimp! I should have thought he'd be man enough to respond to both compliments *and* complaints.

An important part of artful listening is to know when to stop listening. At some point the leader must either make a decision himself or delegate it to someone else, and then move on. The good news is that listening carefully and intensively at the beginning can save the leader a lot of time at the end. Indeed, as we'll see in a later chapter, artful listening is a key element in stretching the leader's time and effectiveness.

Just as one can think gray without ever needing to reach a conclusion, one can listen gray without ever needing to deliver a response. Sometimes a response is not really necessary, and sometimes no response at all is the best response.

One final aspect of listening gray is that a leader shouldn't make up his mind about people's credibility unless and until he has to. Many failed leaders felt they had to decide right away whether someone was worth listening to. They tended to write off apparent fools, only to find that inarticulate people sometimes have the most valuable things to say. I'm often amazed at how easily some would-be leaders are taken in by glib, highly educated idiots, while dismissing out of hand deep thinkers who find it difficult to put their thoughts into words. The key is to not rush to a conclusion—either about what you hear, or from whom you hear it.

Various observers have said that Eckhard Pfeiffer's tenure as CEO of Compaq ended abruptly in significant part because of his

listen to all

tendency to divide people into an A-list to whom he listened, and a B-list to whom he paid little or no attention. When he set the company on course to become a leader in e-business, his inability to hear the good ideas of B-list people resulted in a loss of direction and a loss of confidence that in turn resulted in Pfeiffer's startlingly swift fall from grace.

I'm an enthusiastic proponent of open communication in an organization as a means of cutting through the swampy bog of bureaucracy. I appreciate having the freedom to talk informally to employees and colleagues over a wide range of levels in the hierarchy—freely giving and receiving ideas and opinions about what we do at USC and the people we serve.

The danger here is one of undercutting the authority and responsibility of line administrators and managers. As I noted earlier, it's very easy for a leader to inadvertently change the de facto reporting relationship of a person several layers down in the organization, simply by the leader's talking directly to that person. In my experience the best way to walk this tightrope is through something I call "open communication with structured decision making." Under this rubric, everyone in the organization is free to communicate directly with everyone else in the organization, with the explicit caveat that *any and all commitments, allocations, and decisions will be made strictly through the hierarchy.*

What does this mean in practice? It means that I can talk directly with any department chair or faculty member or nonacademic manager I please without going through the intervening layers of authority, and similarly anyone in the organization can communicate directly with me or with any senior vice president or dean. Sounds simple, doesn't it? It is in theory, but it only works if everyone understands and accepts the second half of the equation—*structured decision making.*

Let's take an example. Suppose a distinguished professor calls me to complain about the egregious sins of his department chair. I listen closely and ask questions until I fully understand the points he's trying to make. He then might ask me what changes *I'm* going to make or directives *I'm* going to issue in order to fix the problem, and I reply, "None." "What?" he asks, "you're not going to take things in hand yourself and address my grievances?" And I say, "Look, Professor, you've explained the problem to me in great detail, and I've listened carefully and fully understand your point of view. I will faithfully report what you've told me to the provost, who I'm sure will discuss it at great length with the dean, who in turn will undoubtedly discuss it with the chairman of your department. But I hire and fire the provost, not the department chairs. I could, if I chose, reach down through our bureaucracy and directly manipulate budgets and appointments in your department, but I strictly adhere to the rule of *structured decision making*. Indeed, if I were to do otherwise, your and my freedom to talk directly to each other without fear of reprisal or rebellion would almost certainly be curtailed."

A friend of mine, who is an extraordinarily successful business leader and entrepreneur, once took issue with me about the concept of open communication with structured decision making. He told me of an experience he had had in which he stopped by the laboratory of one of the engineers in his company to see what was going on and ask a few questions. A few days later the manager of that division complained to my friend that he had redirected the work in that engineer's laboratory. My friend felt terrible about it. "All I did," he said, "was ask a few questions." But what he didn't realize was that he has a well-deserved reputation as a hands-on CEO. The engineer had misinterpreted my friend's innocent questions as a directive from the big boss to change direction. Once again, open communication only works if the other half of the bargain, structured decision making, is strictly and faithfully adhered to.

Artful listening can provide unexpected leverage, something which was demonstrated many times by an old friend of mine, Sam Regenstrief. Sam had retained me as an engineering consultant to his dishwasher manufacturing company, located in a small town in southern Indiana. At one time this company was shipping six thousand dishwashers a day under thirteen different brand labels, which represented a 40 percent market share of all the dishwashers being built in the United States.

Sam was brilliant, but he certainly didn't come across that way on first meeting. He had poor vision, which was corrected with awkward-looking Coke-bottle eyeglasses, and he suffered from a kind of verbal dyslexia. These characteristics often led people we negotiated with (especially those in major cities) to think they were dealing with a naïve bumpkin who was ripe for plucking.

During negotiations Sam would bombard the other side with seemingly stupid questions and would often ask people to repeat things. He seemed to get things mixed up and often appeared befuddled. Frustrated by this time-consuming, roundabout route to consensus, the other side would almost always revise the deal more and more to our liking.

Sam's power as a negotiator came not from an aggressive, take-charge approach, but rather from his ability to spend inordinate amounts of time asking for clarifications and listening to others' demands. He disarmed people with his confused and confusing approach. They thought he wasn't listening at all, while in fact he was always the most artful listener in the room.

Most university presidents, Fortune 500 CEOs or heads of state can't afford to come across as bumpkins. Nonetheless, I learned a great deal from Sam which has proven useful to me over the years. When I'm involved in a tough negotiation I often hold back, take what the other side says in bits, go off in a tangential direction when the pressure is on, and then circle back to the main topic from a fresh perspective. I never say, "No, absolutely not," or "This isn't negotiable." I stay flexible, ask people to tell me more, and listen carefully for a hint of softening or change in the other side.

Conventional wisdom tells us that once an outside person has been named to lead an organization, he should seize the reins of power as quickly as possible. This may be good advice if the organization is in crisis and about to go under, which is often the case when an outsider is named to head a profit-seeking corporation. But in other cases, the newly named leader from the outside would be wise to insist on a period of a few months between the announcement of his appointment and the time at which he actually takes office. During this interregnum he can listen and question and listen some more without any responsibility for making any decisions whatsoever. Everyone within the organization will want to bare his soul to the CEO-elect during this period. And never again will the new leader have a better opportunity to understand the strengths and weaknesses of the organization, the talents of the people in it, and its prospects for the future.

I'm always amazed by the really egregious mistakes that new CEOs make when they come to an organization from the outside. It's not that they're stupid; it's just that they're ignorant. A few months spent in artful listening as the CEO-elect before actually donning the mantle of office would almost guarantee their getting off to a good start.

In my own case I insisted that there be a period of four months between the date on which I was named president of SUNY-Buffalo and the date on which I actually took office in 1982, and I negotiated a similar interregnum during my transition from Buffalo to USC in 1991. If in fact I have been as successful in these two posts as the foreword to this book would have you believe, I attribute much of that success in both cases to my having had the luxury of a long period of artful listening prior to my taking on the responsibilities of leadership.

There are many people in leadership positions who are poor listeners—who care little for what others have to say, or who lack the skills to listen artfully. A few of these people may appear to be very successful. But my guess is that the number of truly effective leaders who have not developed good listening skills is quite small. For the vast majority of us who aspire to excellence in leadership, artful listening isn't just an asset—it's a necessity.

Chapter 3

Experts:
Saviors and Charlatans

It would be difficult to imagine a modern leader practicing his craft without the help of experts. Can we even conceive of someone leading a complex organization today without employing a gaggle of lawyers, scientists, architects, accountants, engineers, and consultants? Of course not.

But what may be less obvious is the large number of leaders who have been brought low by the well-intentioned assistance of experts. So the question is, how can a modern leader use experts to his or her advantage without being used or used up by them?

George Bernard Shaw once said that "every profession is a conspiracy against the laity." He wasn't completely wrong; experts and the professions they represent are not always a boon to mankind.

I once read an article in which the author had marshaled an enormous amount of statistical data to show that it wasn't until 1931 that the medical profession turned the corner, so to speak, and began to do more net good than harm. He contended that, while there were individual doctors and specific procedures prior to 1931 which did much more good than harm, it wasn't until seventy years ago that the profession as a whole began to make a net positive contribution to the health of the public at large. I have no idea whether the author's thesis is correct, but his underlying concept is very appealing. Indeed, I would say intuitively that many professions are still decades away from turning the corner in terms of the net benefits they contribute to society.

I should announce at the outset a conflict of interest that I had in writing this chapter. I've spent essentially all my professional career in the academic community—as a professor, graduate dean, vice president, and president. One of the principal jobs (some would say *the* principal job) of universities is to produce experts and intellectuals. I start out with a bias in favor of such folks because I am one of them. At the same time I know well their warts and shortcomings, which, while not generally egregious, can present serious difficulties for leaders in every part of our society.

So the challenge for me in writing this chapter was to speak lovingly, and yet at the same time candidly, about those of my kith and kin who hold themselves out as having specialized knowledge or intellectual skills not generally available to laymen.

Let me begin with a personal story. One Saturday morning in 1947, when I was seven years old, my father and I drove out together from our farm in Missouri to the county seat. As we climbed out of the car and began walking down the street, I noticed a fairly new building which had been built shortly after the end of World War II. The white exterior of this building was marred by dark yellow and brown streaks running down its surface. In retrospect, I would guess the architect had used ungalvanized steel somewhere in the coping at the top of the walls, which quickly rusted and stained the white sides of the building. Not being able to surmise that at the time, though, I asked my father what had caused "those ugly brown marks." Dad stopped, looked at the building for a long moment, and then looked at me and said, "Son, never trust an architect." And with that he resumed walking.

So far as I know, Dad didn't have it out for architects. In fact he may never have known one personally. And to be fair, the vast majority of architects with whom I've worked throughout the years have been very trustworthy professionals who put their clients' interests first.

But my father's response of half a century ago contains some implicit practical advice for leaders who must deal with experts. To once again paraphrase the philosopher Eric Hoffer: a leader should pay close attention to experts but never take them too seriously, and never ever trust them completely.

By most people's reckoning, Frank Lloyd Wright was a great architect—perhaps the greatest of the twentieth century. But he demanded from his clients a degree of subjugation and a capacity for humiliation that most of us would find unbearable.

In the early 1900s Wright designed a home for Mr. and Mrs. Darwin Martin of Buffalo, New York. This outstanding example of Wright's work became the property of SUNY-Buffalo in the late 1960s. When the university acquired the house it also acquired a great deal of the original correspondence between Wright and Martin. What is clear from these letters is that Wright was an egomaniac of gargantuan proportions who didn't give a damn about his clients' needs or desires. Wright saw his role as that of a creative genius, and the role of the Martins as that of wealthy ignoramuses who were lucky to have the opportunity to live in (and pay for) a Wright-designed house. The upshot was that the entire Martin family (save for the long-suffering Mr. Martin) hated Wright, his house, and his monumental ego.

I spent many wonderful hours in the partially restored Martin House when I was president of SUNY-Buffalo from 1982 to 1991. I could almost feel Wright's presence and creativity in the symphony of interior details, in the beautiful stained-glass windows, and in the few pieces of original Wright-designed furniture still remaining in the house. No doubt about it, the Martin House is an outstanding work of art. But as a home for the Martins it was a dismal failure. Wright was certainly an artistic genius. But was he an architect in the sense of a professional whose first obligation is to serve his client's needs and interests?

Many experts are more interested in serving their own egos, or advancing their own reputations within their guilds or among their professional peers, than in serving their clients. They get around this ethical dilemma by convincing themselves that they know what's good for their client far better than the client knows what's good for himself. Sometimes they're right. But sometimes such experts can achieve such Rasputin-like standing among their clientele that the cowed customers are afraid to even raise a question about what's going on (How *dare* you suggest that the emperor is naked?).

It isn't just architects who are capable of exhibiting this kind of egocentric behavior. Various interior decorators, business consultants, engineers, accountants, lawyers, physicians, software designers and surgeons demonstrate it as well.

A friend of mine told me about his recent struggles with a graphic design firm he had hired to promote a new venture at his university. His staff wanted to use large type in the section headings and photo captions in the brochure because many of their donors are elderly (i.e., over sixty, like me) and find it difficult to read fine print. The graphic designers, on the other hand, insisted that the type for these parts had to be small in order to preserve the "artistic integrity" of the brochure. They were apparently more interested in impressing their professional colleagues around the country (and perhaps winning an award) than they were in getting their client's message across to donors.

As someone who has spent a great deal of time working both as an expert and as a leader, I would agree with Warren Bennis that it's essential for an expert to be a "deep specialist" and for a leader to be a "deep generalist." The expert's role is to offer greater insight than the leader has in one or a small number of areas, while the leader's role is to be sufficiently broad so as to be able to integrate the advice of several experts into a coherent course of action.

In dealing with experts, it's very important for the leader to know precisely what his goals are and how he thinks a particular expert might help him achieve those goals. For example, the principal style of architecture for USC, adopted in the 1920s, is Italian Romanesque. This classic style involves brick walls, decorative arches, colonnades and loggias, and red tile roofs. During my ten years at USC, literally thousands of our constituents—students, faculty, parents, alumni and donors—have told me how much they love the buildings on our campus that reflect this style of architecture, and not a single person has ever said he dislikes them.

In the 1960s USC began to abandon the Italian Romanesque style of architecture in favor of an eclectic collection of modern buildings. Thousands of our constituents have told me how much they dislike these buildings, and not one has ever said he prefers them to our more traditional buildings.

So what architectural style should I, as president of USC, be pushing for today in the face of one of the biggest building booms in our university's history? Should my personal tastes (which lean toward modern) be my guide, or should I try instead to serve some set of higher interests? And if the latter, which higher interests?

The answer, I think, is quite clear. It matters not a whit what architectural style I might personally prefer. All that matters is what style will best advance USC's role and mission.

USC is in the business of teaching, research and public service. To that end we must attract the very best students and faculty and raise a great deal of money to support them. We are decidedly *not* in the business of erecting buildings for their own sake; rather, we build buildings solely to help us carry out our academic mission. And that means erecting buildings which will be genuinely attractive over the long term to the brightest young people and the most outstanding professors, and which will warm the hearts of alumni, donors, parents and friends.

The net result? We are now tearing down some of the more distasteful buildings of the '60s on our campus and replacing them with new buildings in the Italian Romanesque style.

Sometimes there are no higher programmatic interests to be served by a building; sometimes the building itself *is* all that matters. A good example is Frank Gehry's new Guggenheim Museum in Bilbao, Spain. I've never met anyone who seriously believed that the Guggenheim in New York would release an appreciable fraction of its most important holdings to a satellite museum in a small and relatively inaccessible city in northern Spain. So in choosing an architect for the new museum, the town fathers of Bilbao understood an important point: *the building itself* would have to be sufficiently stunning and original to attract tourists from around the world. It was a risky gamble, but one that has paid off handsomely for Bilbao. People can argue for years to come as to whether or not Gehry's creation is a good art museum, but almost everyone agrees that it is, in and of itself, an outstanding work of art, and that it is worth a trip to Bilbao to see it.

Sydney, Australia, won a similar gamble with its opera house, which is a maintenance nightmare but a beautiful international icon for both Sydney and Australia. By contrast, the Australian national government lost out completely when it built its new capitol building in Canberra, which is just another funny-looking structure that has never become a symbol for anything.

I'm always astounded by the extent of the herd instinct within the artistic professions. You might expect a high degree of conformity among such prosaic practitioners as doctors, engineers and accountants, but wouldn't you think that clothing designers, filmmakers, painters, musicians, architects and writers would be militantly individualistic? The very best are, of course, but most of the rest are slaves to fashion.

Now, buying a dress or a piece of art that falls out of fashion in a few years is no big deal; you can always hide it in your closet or give it to Goodwill. But buildings that reflect a short-term fad are a much bigger problem. They're physically designed to last for decades (and sometimes centuries), so it's much harder to hide them when they become outdated or ugly due to changing fashions. Thus, dealing with architects presents a special challenge for any leader, because his mistakes in this arena will be around for a long time to come.

Our age has often been called the Age of Science. But it's really the Age of Scientific Technology, a seemingly innocuous nuance that has major implications for today's leaders. As science and technology become more pervasive in the life of every organization, it becomes increasingly important for leaders to thoroughly understand the distinctions and symbiotic relationships between the two. In fact in the twenty-first century, scientific and technological experts may prove to be the most important members of any leader's stable of advisers.

Some readers who lack technical backgrounds may be inclined to skip this section. Please don't; it touches on a number of essential aspects of contrarian leadership. Moreover, I think you'll find it to be both interesting and accessible.

As a general rule, leaders are much more interested in technology than they are in science. That's because technology allows leaders to exploit the natural world for their own ends—to manipulate the course of events in accordance with the leader's desires. Science, on the other hand, is more concerned with *understanding* the natural world, which on its face is of relatively little interest to leaders.

But over the past two centuries, and especially over the past sixty years, science and technology have become increasingly intertwined, so much so that it's hard for most leaders today to tell them apart.

Such has not always been the case; indeed for most of human history, science and technology have been completely separate enterprises. Technology was alive and well for hundreds of thousands of years before the birth of science, and continued to prosper independently for more than two millennia while science was still in its infancy. Clubs, axes, spears, the bow and arrow, swords, fire, pottery, baskets, fabric, the wheel-and-axle, writing, agriculture, domesticated animals, fermentation, buildings, bronze, iron, steel, gunpowder, medicine, surgery, sailing ships, mirrors, paper, the printing press—all are technologies that were initially developed by mankind through trial and error with essentially no assistance from science. One does not need to understand *why* the foregoing technologies work in order to use them; rather, a simple recipe is sufficient (e.g., mix three parts molten copper with one part molten tin, let it cool, and zingo—you get bronze).

By contrast, science, in the sense of quantitative predictive theories based on careful observations and coherent explanations of physical phenomena, had its beginnings in ancient Greece a mere 2,500 years ago, and promptly went into eclipse for nearly a thousand years with the fall of the Roman Empire. From the outset, science was essentially irrelevant to technology and therefore irrelevant to leaders as well. Initially, science produced its most innovative results in the seemingly useless field of astronomy. Even the spectacular success in the seventeenth century of Newton's laws in explaining the motions of the planets around the sun had relatively little effect on either technology or leaders.

With few exceptions it wasn't until the nineteenth century that science and technology began to seriously join forces. It was something of an on-again, off-again partnership; even at the beginning of the twentieth century, many of the world's most prolific inventors, including Thomas Edison, were openly contemptuous of science and scientists, as were most leaders of government, industry and the military.

Nonetheless, and however haltingly, science and technology have become bedfellows over the past two hundred years, and the fruits of that union have been growing exponentially in both number and importance with each passing decade. For leaders, the implications of this sea change in the relationship between science and technology are enormous. Today, scientific research actually *begets* new technologies that would never have been discovered through the trial-and-error methods which have historically been the basis of most technological developments. This new reality has kindled among many leaders a newfound interest in scientific research.

The power of modern science lies in the concept of falsification; that is, any scientific theory someone might propose is as good as any other theory unless or until there is experimental evidence to the contrary. Thus, in the modern scientific tradition, one does not "prove" a theory; rather, one can only disprove it. As Albert Einstein observed, "No amount of experimentation can prove me right; a single experiment can prove me wrong." But until the theory is in fact disproved or falsified, until it's found to be at odds with experimental evidence, it's accepted as being true. In a sense, then, scientific theories live in a Darwinian world in which each is vulnerable to extinction at any moment.

Now here's the key point for leaders (and managers too, for that matter): it's not important whether a particular scientific theory is really "true" in some ultimate sense; rather, what counts to leaders are the practical technologies that can be wrung from that theory. Scientific theories may come and go, but technologies and calculations based on those theories are still usable within the limits of validity of the underlying theories themselves. Even when a theory (such as Newton's law of gravitation) has been falsified in the strict sense, it can still be used to great advantage (but within specific limits) for making calculations and solving practical technological problems.

Thus science and technology over the past sixty years have become, and continue to become, more and more tightly fused together. Many scientists are in fact technologists, in that their research is directed toward developing a specific drug or device. A good case in point is the transistor, which was invented in the late 1940s, not by engineers, but by three physicists at Bell Labs who were ultimately awarded the Nobel Prize in physics for their achievement. Similarly, many engineers today are doing applied (or even basic) science, because it is often necessary to gain a deeper understanding of a physical phenomenon before it can be technologically exploited.

Where does all this leave the leader? Provided he's working with experts and technologies in the so-called "hard" or natural sciences (e.g., physics, chemistry, and biology), in which theories can be readily falsified and delimited in terms of their validity, there's no great danger of his being grossly misled. He might of course lose a lot of money by investing in a new *technology* which proves to be too expensive or otherwise impractical in the marketplace. But the chances of his being hoodwinked on the basis of totally false scientific premises are very small.

The natural sciences and their attendant technologies play an increasingly important role in every aspect of modern life. Whether he would or not, every leader needs to be sufficiently conversant with these areas of human endeavor so he can choose his scientific and technological experts wisely and use them profitably.

My friend Warren Bennis believes that, while only a tiny fraction of the population are practicing physical scientists, essentially everyone is a practicing social scientist. At the risk of being overly picky, I might substitute the term "social technologist" for "social scientist" here. But it's certainly true that all of us from an early age develop theories as to how people and society work, and how we might best navigate the shoals of social intercourse to our advantage.

But what about the social sciences as *science*? How does one go about falsifying theories in these disciplines? And are there social technologies based on the social sciences which might prove useful to a leader?

Many people, especially in the natural sciences, argue that the social sciences are not science at all because their theories are not readily subjectable to falsification. It's difficult to fashion a clear and unambiguous prediction based on a social-science theory in such a way that the prediction can then be readily tested for falsity by other social scientists around the world.

Social scientists spend a lot of time arguing over definitions of terms, and how one should go about measuring the quantities encompassed by those terms, and what instruments and units one should use in making those measurements. By contrast, natural scientists and engineers spend relatively little time squabbling over such matters. As a consequence, a really silly theory in the natural sciences can often be discredited in a matter of a year or so, whereas it might take a century to convincingly falsify a theory in the social sciences.

For example, let us compare the discrediting of cold fusion in physics with the ultimate rejection of Freudianism in psychology. Stanley Pons of the University of Utah and Martin Fleischmann of the University of Southampton stunned the world on March 23, 1989, by announcing they had succeeded in producing nuclear fusion at room temperature in a jar on a desktop. Within days their "discovery" was headline news around the world. But also within days other scientists began to try to duplicate Pons and Fleischmann's experiments in their own laboratories. A few reported encouraging results, but most did not.

Within a few months the weight of scientific opinion began to turn against cold fusion, not out of peevishness or jealousy, but because the theory of cold fusion made predictions which were being contradicted by experiments all over the world. Pons and Fleischmann became pariahs in the scientific community, the president of the University of Utah resigned, and the matter came to a close.

Now let's look at Freud. He first published his theory of the interpretation of dreams in 1899, his landmark *Origin and Development of Psychoanalysis* in 1910, and his theory of the id, the ego and the superego in 1923. Did Freud's theories make predictions? Yes, sort of. Were they subject to falsification by experiment, using agreed-upon definitions and methods of measurement? No.

In actual fact, Freud's terms were so fuzzy and his methods of measurement were so ill-defined that his theories could be used to explain almost any psychological behavior. But what they couldn't do was make predictions which could be readily and unambiguously subjected to the test of falsification through experiments conducted by other psychologists around the world.

So by wrapping Freud's psychological theories in the mantle of real science, with its dictum that any theory is true unless and until it's falsified by experiment, Freud's disciples were able to maintain the "truth" of his theories for nearly a hundred years. In fact, it wasn't until the development and widespread use of several psychotropic ethical drugs in the 1990s that Freud's feet of clay were fully exposed.

All right, granted, many theories in the social sciences may not be as reliable as those in the natural sciences because the former don't make predictions that are readily subjectable to falsification. But what about technologies based on the social sciences? Mightn't some of these be useful to a modern leader?

The answer is: yes, but be very, very careful. Hitler pursued monstrously evil ends through the use of social technologies based on social-science theories. Hundreds of other leaders in the century just past employed social-science theories as justifications for using repressive social technologies against ethnic and religious minorities and women. And it was social technologists who removed phonics from the schools, told us cocaine was not really addictive, and tried to convince us that broken homes are just as good for kids as whole ones, all allegedly on the basis of social-science research.

On the other hand, the IQ test is a good example of a useful social technology that is based on a social-science theory which I suspect is simply silly: to wit, that there is in each person's brain a single region or software construct which constitutes that person's general intelligence, and that that single construct can be characterized by a single number, and that that single number can be measured through a simple written test. Most of the leaders I've known believe that the foregoing theory is errant nonsense. But many of these same leaders also believe that IQ tests can be useful screening tools. Such tests can help identify those people who will probably do well in certain jobs or situations and those who will probably do poorly. Most leaders also understand that such tests can under certain circumstances be very misleading, and can even on occasion damage the lives and careers of some of the people being tested. And finally, most leaders understand that an IQ test doesn't really measure a person's intrinsic intelligence, but simply measures that person's performance on the IQ test itself.

Of course, technologies based on the natural sciences can also be dangerous and counterproductive. Which leaders were smart enough to foresee the havoc that would be wreaked upon our environment through the widespread use of internal combustion engines, or the fact that hair spray and refrigerators could put a hole in the ozone layer that would lead to increased skin cancer in the southern hemisphere, or that television could numb the minds of a whole generation of young people?

The point is, all technologies, be they social or physical, are potentially useful and potentially dangerous; all have the possibility of producing salutary effects and harmful side effects. The difference for the leader is that, in the case of technologies based on the natural sciences, he can at least be comforted by the fact that the underlying science has either withstood the test of ruthless efforts at falsification, or been clearly delimited thereby, while such is not the case with most technologies based on the social sciences. That may be the reason why so many effective leaders wisely rely as much on custom and judgment as they do on social-science research in evaluating proposals for new social technologies.

All of which is not to say that the social sciences are somehow inferior to the natural sciences, any more than the arts and humanities are. Leaders must simply keep in mind that, in most instances, the social sciences are a radically different animal from the natural sciences.

In many ways the social sciences rise above the natural sciences to the level of poetry and myth; as such, they provide us with ways for making sense of the world around us which transcend the cold realities and limited applicability of the natural sciences. As Ralph Ellison observed, "Man without myth is like Othello without Desdemona: chaos descends, faith vanishes, and superstitions prowl in the mind. . . . It is the creative function of myth to protect the individual from the irrational." And as the quintessential natural scientist himself, Albert Einstein, once noted, "A lot of what can be counted doesn't count, and a lot of what counts can't be counted."

Thus there is a great deal which any leader can glean from the social sciences, provided he is careful not to confuse them with the natural sciences.

We now come to a group of experts who are dear to the heart of every leader: lawyers. This bond of affection is especially strong in the United States, which has more practicing lawyers and lawsuits per capita than any other industrialized nation.

Let's start our contrarian analysis of lawyers by first taking a look at the peculiarities of the law itself. The Constitution of the United States contains an explicit prohibition against *ex post facto* laws—that is, laws which retroactively prohibit a certain behavior. European monarchs would sometimes use such laws to have a person arrested and tried for having committed a crime which wasn't a crime at the time the person committed it. The Founding Fathers wanted none of that in America!

But that's exactly what we have today in this country, thanks to decisions by judges and juries which declare, after the fact, that certain acts are "illegal" (i.e., punishable by large "fines" in the form of judgments), when no law explicitly forbade such acts, and when no reasonable person would have thought such acts were illegal at the time they were committed.

An excellent example of this kind of legislation-by-jury is the case of a New Mexico woman who was awarded $2.7 million (later reduced to $640,000) for having burned herself with a hot cup of coffee which she had purchased at a McDonald's restaurant. The case drew national attention because of the breathtaking irrationality of the decision—after all, the plaintiff knew the coffee was very hot, and yet had chosen to place the coffee cup between her legs while attempting to drive her car. It was thrilling (and a little frightening) that twelve everyday citizens in New

Mexico, whom no one had elected to anything, could arbitrarily and capriciously pass a sweeping new "hot coffee law" that applied, for all intents and purposes, to 260 million Americans.

Do we look to Congress and our state legislatures any more for dramatic and surprising new laws? No, we look instead to the judiciary. "It's a sign of the times that reformers now routinely skip the legislative process and take their issues directly to court," *U.S. News and World Report* columnist John Leo observed several years ago. Even more recently, former Harvard University president Derek Bok offered this chilling assessment: "The United States has already gone further than any other country in allowing the courts to make decisions that are the prerogative of elected officials in other democratic nations."

Indeed, over the last fifty years, a substantial fraction of the really important new legislation in America—affecting everything from asbestos to tobacco—has come from the secret deliberations of juries and the pens of appointed judges, rather than from the collective voice of elected legislators. It's no wonder that the single most important question which many Americans ask themselves about a presidential candidate these days is, "What kind of people will he appoint to the Supreme Court?"

Personally, I think this trend toward legislation by the courts is unhealthy. But that's neither here nor there. The relevant point for contrarian leaders is this: neither you nor your lawyers can know with any certainty what the law is today, because the law can at any time be modified retroactively by the courts.

At USC my senior advisers and I spend a significant amount of time with attorneys, trying to figure out what we can do legally and what we can't. It's generally not so much a question of reading law and precedents as it is trying to predict the behavior of judges and juries.

This game has become so sophisticated that some people now make a business of selecting mock juries comprised of persons who are drawn from, and statistically representative of, the citizens in the jurisdiction in which their client's case will be tried, and then conducting a mock trial using this mock jury. This form of games-manship simply underscores the fact that, from a practical stand-point, the laws of California and of the United States are not necessarily the same in San Diego as they are a hundred miles north in Los Angeles.

A leader should always be suspicious when a lawyer, or any expert for that matter, says a concept or strategy is just too com-plicated for the expert to explain to the leader. I've always believed that a physicist who can't say something intelligible about quantum mechanics to a bright twelve-year-old simply doesn't understand quantum mechanics himself. The same rule of thumb applies to lawyers.

Of course, every leader depends explicitly on his lawyers to read and synthesize the statutes, case law and regulations applic-able to a particular case, and then interpret this synthesis to the leader and his lieutenants. But sometimes it's helpful for a leader and his advisers to read the law themselves, and reach their own preliminary conclusions without having any lawyers present. I've been amazed at the fresh approaches to a legal conundrum that can be generated in this manner (an example of thinking free, à la Chapter 1).

A few years ago a national magazine published a story by a freelance journalist that contained a number of scurrilous asser-tions about USC which were patently false. I was furious! Our attorneys assured us we had an open-and-shut case against the magazine for libel, especially since the publisher was based on the East Coast and the case would be tried before a Los Angeles jury.

My board of trustees agreed from the outset that the decision as to whether or not we should file suit was strictly up to me. But several of the older and wiser heads on the board urged me not to do it. It wasn't that they thought we'd lose the suit; it was that they understood better than I that the issue at hand was political, not legal, and that the aftermath of beating the bad guys in court might well be worse than the relatively minor injury we had sustained at the hands of an unethical publisher and an unscrupulous journalist. In the end I listened to my trustee colleagues and rejected the advice of the legal experts.

Experts, God love 'em, are as necessary to the modern leader as cellular telephones and e-mail. And they're all out there eagerly awaiting calls from leaders to come in and be of assistance. The question is, whom should you call and what exactly should you ask them to do?

It helps to know what it is you hope to get out of an expert before you ask him to become a part of your team. And because his knowledge and expertise are esoteric relative to your own, it helps to develop mutual sympathy and trust between you and the expert before going too far down the garden path together. Finally, it's very important that the expert be able and willing to explain to you, in terms you can understand, everything he's doing or plans to do.

Experts, for their part, need to be able to see themselves as bona fide partners of the leaders and organizations that employ them. When the experts themselves can practice artful listening, they are much better able to understand the true objectives of the leader and contribute to the achievement of those objectives.

I myself was a practicing expert (as a consulting engineer) for a number of years. I *almost* always put my client's interests first, and *almost* never let my ego get the better of me. But as I look back, I can see that those of my clients who benefited most from my services were leaders who never became too dependent on me, who always maintained their intellectual independence, and who never kidded themselves that expertise could be a substitute for leadership.

Chapter 4

You Are What You Read

To a greater extent than we realize, and to a far greater extent than we would ever care to admit, we are what we read.

For some of us, reading is a way to gain perspective and stimulate original thinking. But for most people reading is simply a form of entertainment, or worse, an insidious means by which they lose their intellectual independence.

Suppose a leader were forced to choose between reading the *New York Times* on a particular day and reading Machiavelli's masterwork *The Prince*. Conventional wisdom would favor the *Times* by a country mile. After all, today's *Times* is fresh and new, while Machiavelli's little handbook is stale and old. And besides, the leader in question may have already read *The Prince* twenty years ago while he was in college.

But contrarian wisdom argues just the opposite. As we shall see in this chapter, a leader can miss a day or a week or even several months of the daily newspapers and be none the worse for it, and in some cases even be the better for it. But missing an opportunity to read or reread Machiavelli (or any of the other supertexts we'll take note of later) could be a major loss for both the leader and his followers.

When Warren Bennis and I teach our course on leadership each spring, we always take a little flak from some of our students for having included *The Prince* as one of the five required texts for the course. Remember that the forty students in this class are handpicked from among USC's brightest and most ambitious upperclassmen, and most of them have already demonstrated considerable leadership skills during their first few years in college. They frequently ask, "What in the world can an obscure Florentine bureaucrat who's been dead for nearly five hundred years have to say that's relevant to leadership in the twenty-first century?"

In response, I go to the board and say, "OK, let's make a list of all the texts in the whole world which are four hundred years old or more and are still widely read today." The first five are easy: the Judeo-Christian Bible, the Qur'an, the Bhagavad Gita, the Pali Canon of Buddhism, and the Analects of Confucius. Then, in rapid succession, nearly everyone agrees to include Plato's *Republic*, Aristotle's *Politics*, the plays of Shakespeare, the plays of Sophocles, Dante's *Divine Comedy*, Homer's *Iliad* and *Odyssey*, Montaigne's *Essays*, Cervantes's *Don Quixote*, and of course Machiavelli's *The Prince* (of which there are more than fifty editions currently in print in the United States alone). After that, consensus becomes more difficult to achieve: perhaps the Upanishads should be included, perhaps Virgil's *Aeneid*, perhaps the plays of Aeschylus, perhaps something of Plutarch, perhaps *Beowulf* or *Chanson de Roland* or Chaucer's *Canterbury Tales* or Maimonides' *Guide to the Perplexed* or More's *Utopia*.

The point is not whether the list contains twelve or twenty-four or even fifty entries; rather, the point is that the list is extremely *short*. Think of it: of all the hundreds of thousands of books, essays, poems, letters, plays and histories that were composed four hundred years ago or more, only a dozen or two are still widely read today.

"Now," I say to my students, "what influence do you think these one or two dozen supertexts have had on the course of human history? How do you think they have shaped the way people have thought, written, spoken and acted over the past several centuries, up to and including today?"

Of course the answer is obvious: these supertexts have had, and continue to have, an enormous influence on every part of our culture. Anyone who in 2001 writes a book or an article or a poem or a play, or makes a movie, or gives a speech, is influenced far more than he knows by these supertexts, even if he has never read them or even *heard* of them.

Why is that? What gives these supertexts such great power? Is it because they're especially well written and insightful? Perhaps. But from the standpoint of their usefulness to leaders, it doesn't matter whether these supertexts are great literature or not. Rather, all that matters is the fact that each has been widely read for the last four hundred years or more and is therefore part of the very foundation of our culture.

Let's put this special power in perspective. Almost everything that's written in the world today (e.g., letters, memos, e-mails) is read by one or a few people and then discarded. Even a front-page story in the *Los Angeles Times,* which might be read (or at least scanned) by as many as a million people, has essentially no readers twenty-four hours after it hits the streets. For a scientific or scholarly article to be read by as many as thirty people five years after it was published is extraordinary. And fewer than one in two hundred of all books published in the United States are still in print and being purchased ten years after they first appeared in the bookstores.

So to write something—anything at all—that is still read by even a small audience fifty years later is a major achievement. And to leave a written legacy that is still widely read after four or more centuries is almost inconceivably rare—*and* influential.

In these tempestuous times it often appears that everything is changing, and changing at an increasingly rapid rate. In such an environment a leader can gain a tremendous competitive advantage by being able to discern the few things that are not changing at all, or changing only slowly and slightly. And nothing can help him do that better than developing a close relationship with a few of the supertexts.

Willa Cather once remarked that "there are only two or three human stories, and they go on repeating themselves as fiercely as if they had never happened before." I might expand Cather's number to half a dozen, but no more. And all of these stories are eloquently told and retold in the supertexts. For example, the story of how King David committed adultery with Bathsheba, and then arranged to have her husband killed so David could marry her and cover up the fruits of their adultery, is absolutely timeless. So are the characterizations of introspective Hamlet and brave Antigone, and so is the advice that Machiavelli gives to would-be leaders.

An important point to keep in mind is that the supertexts are not infallible (unless, of course, one's religious beliefs dictate otherwise). Every leader must make his own decisions concerning the validity or applicability of a particular passage in a particular text. For example, I think Machiavelli was myopic in concluding that followers could only love, fear or hate their leaders. In point of fact, numerous people throughout history, and especially in the past three hundred years, have effectively led others by gaining the *respect* of their followers.

I'm sometimes asked to identify those of the supertexts which in my opinion are the most valuable for modern leaders. After *The Prince*, I would choose the stories of four of the greatest leaders in the Bible: Moses (in the book of Exodus), David (in 1 and 2 Samuel), Jesus (in Matthew) and Paul (in Acts). Next on my list would be: Plato's *Republic* for the way it brings out the best in us; Shakespeare's *Hamlet* for giving us a terrifying look inside ourselves, and his *Othello* for a view of a leader undone by an evil lieutenant; Sophocles' *Antigone* to help us see the pitfalls of rigidity in a leader; and all of John Ciardi's translation of Dante's *Divine Comedy* for its portrayal of the full range of human triumphs and foibles.

The key contribution of the supertexts is not a set of timeless truths about leadership, but rather some timeless truths about human nature. One of the great fallacies of our age (and perhaps of any age) is the belief that we are fundamentally different from our ancient forebears, that we have somehow outgrown the barbaric and benighted practices of centuries and millennia past. What nonsense! We are every bit as human, and no more human, than the characters in the Old Testament or the people of sixteenth-century Florence. I'm not suggesting that we are constrained to act or talk or even think the same way as those who came before us, but I am saying that our basic natures—our human potentialities, if you will—are identical to theirs. And the supertexts, more than contemporary literature, do an excellent job of helping us understand this timelessness of human nature.

Moreover, the supertexts are important not only for what they say but also for how they say it. Because these texts have been read by so many people over such a long period of time, they have exerted, and continue to exert, an extraordinary influence on the language used by effective leaders, often unbeknownst to the leader himself.

A leader's choices of vocabulary, metaphors, syntax, phraseology and patterns of speech are all affected to a greater or lesser extent by the supertexts, because the leader knows (or unconsciously senses) that the language of these texts (updated with a bit of current jargon) has a high probability of resonating with his followers. Both the leader and his followers have been preprogrammed to some extent by the ideas contained within the supertexts *and* by the language with which those ideas are expressed.

For native speakers of English, the most powerful supertexts in this regard are the King James version of the Bible and the plays of Shakespeare. The influence of these particular texts on the speeches and writing of Lincoln, Franklin Roosevelt and Churchill is almost palpable. Unfortunately, the King James Bible has been mostly replaced by politically correct revisions which seem to lack the power to shape and influence the language of leadership.

Like most people, I enjoy newspapers. I try to scan both the *Los Angeles Times* and the *Wall Street Journal* every day, and when traveling I often read the *New York Times* as a treat.

A free and unfettered press is an absolutely essential element of our form of democratic government. Even though this absolute freedom often does a lot of harm to innocent people and institutions, and even though it may cause the public as a whole to be misled from time to time, I wouldn't trade it or modify it for all the money in the world.

Nonetheless, the popular news media present special problems for every leader. Thomas Jefferson understood this point when he remarked in a letter to John Norville, "The man who never looks into a newspaper is better informed than he who reads them, inasmuch as he who knows nothing is nearer to the truth than he whose mind is filled with falsehoods and errors. He who reads nothing will still learn the great facts, and the details are all false." This remark was later polished into the well-known maxim: "The man who reads nothing at all is better informed than the man who reads nothing but newspapers."

We in the twenty-first century may be tempted to dismiss Jefferson's maxim as a bit of hyperbolic spleen-venting by a leader who lived two centuries ago in a backwater country that was plagued by irresponsible journalists. Surely his remark has no applicability today, when essentially all of our news media are staffed by graduates of professional schools of journalism. Or does it?

In the mid-1980s, when I was president of SUNY-Buffalo, I decided to test Jefferson's maxim in a modern context. Without telling anyone other than my wife, I stopped reading all newspapers and newsmagazines for a period of six months. I also watched no television news during this period (which was no real sacrifice, since I had essentially stopped watching all TV except sports and public television several years before).

I undertook this experiment in order to see what deleterious effects, if any, my being insulated from the popular news media would have on my ability to carry out my responsibilities as the leader of a large and complex institution. I was of course prepared to stop the experiment at any time if I felt my job or the university were suffering from it.

The first two weeks of this experiment were *tough*! They reminded me of the painful two-week period I went through many years before when I quit smoking for good. I *really* wanted to see a newspaper—so much so that I would sneak a peek at the headlines whenever I passed a newsstand, or surreptitiously read what I could when the person sitting in front of me on a plane was perusing a newspaper.

But, as with quitting smoking, after a few weeks I felt a newfound sense of freedom and autonomy. I realized that I (along with nearly everyone else in America) had become addicted to the popular media, and that in so doing I had given over a big chunk of my intellectual independence to a group of editors and reporters whose core values and interests were not necessarily congruent with my own.

Moreover, I was stunned to find that, within twelve hours of a story's first appearing in the popular press, I was often *better* informed about the facts of the story than those of my friends and colleagues who were still addicted to reading newspapers. How could that be? Simple. I was getting my news orally from people (such as my principal advisers) whose biases were well known to me and who had my best interests at heart.

It turns out that people *love* to tell their boss some piece of breaking news which he's not yet heard. A colleague would say to me, "Steve, what do you think of the outbreak of violence in Northern Ireland?" And I'd say, "Gee, John, I haven't had a chance to read the paper this morning. Tell me about it." Which he would then proceed to do with gusto. Only he wouldn't just recite that morning's *New York Times* article on the subject; rather, he would combine the *Times* rendition of the story with those of the *Wall Street Journal*, the *Washington Post*, the *Buffalo News* and CNN, and would then filter this combination through his personal passions and prejudices (with which I was intimately familiar) and apply his own good judgment to come up with what he believed was a true account of the incident in question.

I am by nature an artful listener, so after two or three people had told me about the news of the day I generally had a more complete and accurate picture of what was going on than any of my colleagues or competitors. Granted, this method of getting the news wasn't as efficient as scanning a newspaper, but it was far superior in terms of quality of content. And it really helped me maintain my intellectual independence, so I could decide for myself what was and wasn't important.

That's one of the hidden problems with the popular news media: the fact that we let others decide for us what we should pay attention to and what we should ignore. It isn't just the text of a news story that can mislead us; it's also the choice of which stories get covered at all, and by whom, and where they're placed in the paper (e.g., on page 1 or page 42, above the fold or below, with a one-column headline or across four columns), and whether or not a particular story is accompanied by photographs, and if so, by how many and which ones.

I know scores of leaders who really believe that if a story isn't being covered in section A of the *New York Times*, it isn't worth their knowing about it. To see how silly an approach this is, you need only read the *New York Times* from, say, fifty years ago and ask yourself whether the events that ultimately proved to be important in the long run were consistently receiving prominent coverage at that time. Were there front-page articles in 1951 on Vietnam, school segregation, transistors, computers, space exploration, air pollution, organ transplants, gender discrimination or Middle East oil? Occasionally, perhaps, but for the most part the coverage focused on stories of more ephemeral interest, just as it does today.

I'm not blaming the newspapers here. That's their job—to inform us of day-to-day events, to entertain us, to reflect the public moods and sentiments of the moment, to print stories that will interest us today and that we will *want* to read.

There is, unfortunately, a strong herd instinct in the news media, just as there is in the fashion and entertainment industries. Of course, every individual newspaper has a distinctive herd mentality (e.g., liberal or conservative) within its own newsroom or on its editorial page. But there is also a herd mentality within the journalistic community as a whole. This tendency toward conformity among the media represents a very real danger for leaders. I'm reminded here of a comment made several years ago by a visitor from the Soviet Union, to the effect that, "You Americans are very impressive! You are able to achieve an extraordinary degree of thought control with a free press and no secret police!"

Then too, as Jefferson pointed out, newspapers often get the facts wrong. Everyone I've ever known who happened to be on the inside of a story that was receiving front-page coverage has remarked on this phenomenon. These factual errors are not generally due to malice on the part of the reporter; indeed, often the errors work to the benefit of the people about whom the story is being written. Rather, the errors are usually the result of insufficient time for the reporter to do his research (due to deadlines or a fear of being scooped by a competitor) and/or simple ignorance on the reporter's part.

One of the finest journalists I've ever known once told me that what he likes best about his job is that every few years he gets transferred to a new beat where he knows absolutely nothing about what he's expected to cover. I can understand why this kind of on-the-job training would be especially appealing to anyone with a wide-ranging curiosity, but I can also understand how it might lead to egregious errors and misinterpretations on the reporter's part.

Finally, there's the question of journalistic ethics when it comes to slanting a story in one direction or another.

To be fair, no human being, not even the most disciplined scientist, can begin an investigation without having his mind at least partially made up from the outset. Francis Bacon in the sixteenth century believed that scientists (called natural philosophers in those days) should simply collect observations and facts in a totally neutral way, and that eventually patterns and scientific laws would "leap from the page," so to speak. As it happens, though, Bacon was wrong. Every scientist, and every investigative reporter, starts out with an hypothesis in mind and then tries to collect facts and observations in support of that hypothesis. Neither the scientist nor the reporter is being objective at this point.

But then the ethics of science begin to diverge from those of journalism. A scientist is expected to abandon her hypothesis if the weight of experimental evidence is against it. By contrast, a journalist is ethically free to publish a story based on a discredited hypothesis, provided the story contains no out-and-out fabrications or factual errors. In other words, a journalist is ethically free to cherry-pick among the facts, quotes and data at hand so as to convey to readers an impression that is at odds with the totality of the evidence, while a scientist who did the same thing would be roundly condemned by her peers.

Actually this peculiar (and most would say repugnant) ethical principle in journalism is very valuable in sustaining a democratic form of government. Because it is this principle that allows a journalist to attack a public figure who the journalist *believes* is corrupt, even before the journalist has incontrovertible evidence to support his belief. So long as everything the journalist publishes about his target is true, it's considered ethical journalism, even if to the target himself and to other insiders the published story is obviously a one-sided hatchet job. In this way a reporter can sometimes smoke out a bad actor who is temporarily protected by a thick cloak of respectability. Of course at other times this kind of slanted journalism simply destroys the reputations and careers of people who are for the most part upstanding citizens.

Thus, in the final analysis Jefferson's little maxim is sometimes as true today as it was two centuries ago: the person who in 2001 reads nothing at all may in fact be better informed than the person who reads nothing but newspapers.

Nonetheless, I myself went back to reading newspapers with enthusiasm at the end of my self-imposed six months of abstinence. Let's face it, it's fun to be *au courant* with respect to fashionable thinking, to let editors and reporters direct our attention to this crisis or that problem or this human-interest story on a day-by-day basis. And it is so reassuring to feel that once a story has dropped out of section A in the papers, the problems that gave rise to that story have presumably been solved (e.g., "The famine in Ethiopia must be over because I don't read about it in the papers anymore").

But as a contrarian leader, I'm now a lot more careful about newspapers than I used to be:

- I know that when I read the papers, I do so primarily for entertainment.

- When the papers attack someone, I keep in mind that there may be compelling facts and arguments to that person's credit which the papers are simply ignoring or intentionally downplaying.

- I try to stay aware of the herd mentality that necessarily characterizes each individual newspaper and the media as a whole.

- I try to remember that newspapers are both printed *and written* in black and white; that the last thing a reporter or an editor wants in a story is multiple shades of gray; that most newspaper stories are built around white hats and black hats, virtue and vice, good and evil, all clearly delineated in binary terms.

- I try to keep in mind that the stories that don't make the papers are often more important than the ones that do, that slow but powerful undercurrents in society are the hardest for newspaper people to detect and the most difficult to write about in a compelling way.

- I try to remember, along with Mr. Jefferson, that even the best newspapers often get their facts wrong.

- When there's a story in the papers that's really important to my work as president of USC, I revert to listening to a variety of advisers tell me about it. This is still by far the best way for any leader to get the news he needs to make decisions, assuming his advisers are a diverse group of intelligent people who have the leader's and the institution's best interests at heart and who are willing to tell the leader things he may not want to hear.

Finally, I no longer feel any sense of *duty* about reading the newspapers, and when I don't read them I'm not ashamed to admit it. The newspapers are sort of like soap operas—you can go without seeing them for a few days and come right back in without missing a beat. If I feel I'm becoming too addicted to newspapers, I simply stop reading them altogether for a week or so until I've regained my intellectual independence. It's a great discipline in the Aristotelian sense of bending over backward to correct one's faults.

So far, so good: contrarian leaders read and reread the supertexts as frequently as possible and limit their daily intake of newspapers. But what about the thousands of other publications—books, magazines, journals, trade publications, and the like—that are competing for every leader's attention?

The problem, of course, is lack of time. In my entire life I've never met a leader, whether of a family or a country, who complained of having too much time on his or her hands or too few things to read. On the contrary, most leaders complain of having too many things they want (or feel obligated) to read and too little time in which to read them.

Henry David Thoreau, who spent several hours a day reading at his cabin near Walden Pond, gave this advice: "Read only the best books first, lest there not be time enough to read them all." Thanks, Henry, but how does one determine which are the best?

One approach is to think of all published reading materials as a continuum or spectrum, running from the most ephemeral (newspapers) on the left to the most enduring (the supertexts) on the right. From the standpoint of contrarian leaders, this spectrum reflects increasing importance as one moves from left to right.

Near the newspaper (i.e., left, or least important) end of this spectrum are magazines and trade publications, followed by most (but not all) newly published books. Next we might place journals and other periodicals of substance and a few of the more widely read textbooks. Closer to the supertext (i.e., right, or most important) end of the spectrum would be novels, biographies, plays, histories, poems and essays which are still being read fifty years or more after they were first published.

My editor, upon hearing me make this point, said, "But Dr. Sample, you're arguing against your own book, because it's not fifty years old." Well, yes and no. Put my book up against *The Prince, Hamlet* or *The Republic,* and I lose in a walk. But compare my book to all the *au courant* nonfiction now on the market and it may do pretty well in substantive terms, precisely because it combines practical experience and original thinking with a fairly extensive knowledge of the supertexts. There is always the possibility (albeit very small) that my book will still be read fifty years from now, but until it stands the test of time let's just place it somewhere in the broad mid-range of the spectrum.

The question for each leader then becomes: how much total time do you wish to devote each day to reading (other than digesting memos, letters, e-mail and reports relating directly to your company or institution), and how do you wish to allocate that time across the spectrum of published materials?

Let's start with trade publications. A good rule of thumb for contrarian leaders is to go where your competitors don't go and read what they don't read. Let your lieutenants stay up with the trades; they'll keep you apprised of any important stories in your industry, just as they do with respect to important stories in the newspapers. It breaks my heart to see an ambitious would-be leader trying to move ahead by reading more and more of the routine trade publications in his field. Poor kid—he's wasting his time. Does he really think Warren Buffet and Bill Gates got ahead by slavishly reading the penny press in their respective areas of endeavor?

For the contrarian leader, just one truly original idea is worth a hundred regurgitations of conventional wisdom. And the chances are very high that that one original idea will be stimulated by something the leader reads or hears from *outside* his established field.

So my advice to leaders is to spend relatively less time near the left (newspaper) end of the spectrum and relatively more near the right (supertext) end. In my own case I devote about thirty minutes a day to reading—ten minutes in total for newspapers, trade publications and journals, and twenty minutes for books. And if on any given day I have to reduce my reading time, I always make cuts at the left end of the spectrum.

The good news is that twenty minutes a day translates into 120 hours a year, which allows ample time for me to read a dozen or more long and challenging books each year at a leisurely pace, with plenty of time for thinking through and underlining the more salient passages in each book. Included among my choices in a given year might be two or three of the supertexts (some of which I may have read before), along with several books that have survived the fifty-year test and a few that were published more recently.

Thus in the past three decades I've read nearly four hundred books covering a wide range of history, philosophy, essays, religion, biographies, novels and poetry. Along the way I've gotten a pretty good liberal education, especially for an engineer. Indeed in some ways my education in the liberal arts has been superior to that of my friends who majored in the humanities, because many of them were too young and naïve to appreciate the great books when they read them as students, and most of them never returned to these texts after graduating from college. Moreover, most humanists fail to round out their liberal education by learning anything substantive about science and technology.

A major challenge for me, and for most leaders I should think, is deciding which of the more recently published books we will read each year. There are thousands to choose from, so how should one decide?

We're all constantly being assaulted by friends and colleagues who say something like, "Have you read John Smedley's new book? You haven't? Oh, you simply *must* read it! It's absolutely *fabulous*! You won't be able to put it down! Smedley is clearly one of the great intellectual lights of our age!" The truth is, there is no way of knowing whether Smedley is really one of the great intellectual lights of our age until Smedley (and all the rest of us) have been dead for many years. I'm reminded here of a quote from Winston Churchill: "There is a good saying to the effect that when a new book appears, one should read an old one."

Even (and perhaps especially) literary experts have a hard time picking long-term winners. Look at the Pulitzer and Nobel laureates in literature from the first half of the last century—how many of these are considered today to be among the most important voices of the twentieth century?

I happen to be a passionate aficionado of Willa Cather, who was awarded the Pulitzer Prize in 1923 for her novel *One of Ours*. Hardly anyone today would rank this particular book as one of Cather's major novels. Moreover, as much as I love her and her work, I must admit that few scholars today would say Willa Cather is one of America's leading authors.

One approach that you as a leader might take to this conundrum is to identify a dozen or so candidates among the coterie of recently published books which have been highly recommended by your closest friends and advisers, and then ask each person to spend five minutes discussing his candidate book with you and pointing out some of its best passages. After all, before you spend several hours carefully reading a relatively new book, you deserve a thoughtful preview from a person whose passions and prejudices are familiar to you. In many cases you'll find that this thoughtful preview is all you'll ever want or need to know about that particular book.

All leaders, whether contrarian or otherwise, are heavily influenced by what they read. Indeed, in many cases leaders are directed and inspired as much by their readings as they are by their closest advisers.

Thus the choices a leader makes as to what to read can be crucial in the long run. Moreover, the fact that a leader's time is so limited forces him to make exclusionary choices with respect to his reading. As Thoreau understood so well, reading a newspaper precludes our reading a book, and reading one particular book precludes our reading hundreds of others.

There are no easy or pat responses to this challenge. As with all things touching on leadership, what works for one leader may not work for another, and what works for one leader when he is first starting out may not work for that same leader at a later stage in his career.

But failing to make conscious choices about what to read is one of the worst things a leader can do. It's far better for him to make his own mistakes than it is to permit bestseller lists, editors or literary critics to make his choices for him. No leader worth his salt would let outsiders choose his chief lieutenants for him, and by the same token he shouldn't let someone else choose his books. In reading as in so many other areas, maintaining one's intellectual independence is an essential prerequisite for effective leadership.

Chapter 5

Decisions, Decisions

Decision making is a major element of leadership. It can be fun, exhilarating, an ego trip, a tremendous burden, agonizing, or scary as hell—and sometimes all of the foregoing at once.

Most leaders exercise a significant fraction of their power and authority through the making of decisions. Indeed, one of the tests of a leader's importance is whether anyone is really affected by, or cares about, the decisions he makes. And a leader's legacy is often determined by the long-term effects of his decisions.

Probably the most critical decisions made by leaders relate to the hiring, nurturing and firing of lieutenants. Because this is such a complex and important topic, I deal with it in depth in Chapter 8 ("Work for Those Who Work for You").

When it comes to decision making, the vast majority of us have been brought up with a clean-plate-and-tidy-desk mentality; that is, never put off to tomorrow a decision you can make today. This bit of conventional wisdom may be good counsel for managers and bureaucrats, but it's terrible advice for leaders.

By contrast, the contrarian leader's approach to decision making can be summarized in two general rules:

1. Never make a decision yourself that can reasonably be delegated to a lieutenant.

2. Never make a decision today that can reasonably be put off to tomorrow.

Of course, the weasel word here is *reasonably*. Deciding what that means with respect to a particular impending decision is a fine art requiring a great deal of skill and practice.

Let's begin with Rule 1. Generally speaking, the vast majority of decisions with which a leader is confronted can be reasonably delegated to a lieutenant, provided the leader has excellent lieutenants and is able to choose the one among them who is in the best position to decide a particular issue. But just because a leader can delegate the making of decisions to lieutenants doesn't mean he can avoid taking responsibility for those decisions, especially if things turn out badly as a result.

This is one of the conundrums that prevent most people from becoming effective leaders: they believe (erroneously, as it turns out) that if they have the authority to decide a certain issue, and if in the end they must take personal responsibility for the decision (especially if it proves to be a mistake), then they themselves must personally make the decision. It's simply inconceivable to the average person that he should under any circumstances allow a subordinate to make an erroneous decision for which he (the leader) will be held ultimately responsible. But that is in fact the very essence of major-league leadership.

Military leaders are especially well trained in the art of delegating decisions to subordinates while retaining ultimate responsibility for those decisions. I recall hearing a story (possibly apocryphal) about Secretary of Defense Robert MacNamara during the ill-fated Bay of Pigs invasion of 1961. MacNamara was of course a total amateur when it came to waging war. As he and the joint chiefs of staff were watching a display that showed the positions of the U.S. ships as they approached Cuba, MacNamara noticed that one of the ships had moved out of formation. He immediately asked the chief of staff of the Navy to order the captain of that particular ship to move back into his prescribed position, to which the admiral allegedly replied, "Mr. Secretary, I'll be happy to relieve the fleet commander if you'd like me to, but as long as he's in charge I'm not going to tell him how to direct the individual ships under his command." Unlike his boss, the chief of staff of the Navy understood the realities *and the risks* of high-stakes delegation.

So why should a leader delegate at all? Why not reserve unto himself every possible decision, both large and small? After all, if he's the leader, everyone should be doing what he says, right?

Actually, many leaders of smaller movements and organizations do try to make all the decisions themselves, and under certain circumstances this approach works very well. But such leaders almost always crash and burn as the organization grows; or alternatively, the organization itself collapses when the original leader ages, becomes ill or dies.

Even in small organizations there are compelling reasons why a leader should consistently delegate most decisions to selected ones of his lieutenants. The first has to do with time constraints. Making a good decision is hard, time-consuming work, and no leader can make many good decisions in a month's time, much less in a day or a week. So he needs to carefully reserve for himself only the most important decisions, and cheerfully delegate the rest.

A second major factor in favor of delegation is that it helps develop and nurture strong lieutenants. As we'll see in a later chapter, a leader can't expect his lieutenants to grow and grow up unless he gives them the opportunity to make real decisions that will have real consequences for the organization, without their being constantly second-guessed by the leader.

Jack Welch, the legendary CEO of General Electric, understood this point exceptionally well. At GE under Welch, business decisions involving $25 million or less were made by operating officers, not by the CEO. Welch would listen to a lieutenant who was wrestling with a major decision, ask questions, and perhaps offer a companywide perspective, but he always resisted making the lieutenant's decision for him.

Finally, the contrarian leader who is willing to delegate almost all decisions to lieutenants has an opportunity to build a much stronger and more coherent organization than does the leader who tries to make all the decisions himself. This assertion is very counterintuitive; one would think at first blush that strength and coherence would be on the side of the absolute dictator. But here's the key: the leader who delegates is forced to build coherence by putting together a team of lieutenants who have shared values and common goals. If he's successful in this regard, his organization can survive the loss of the leader himself (which will always happen eventually).

By contrast, when a dictatorial leader leaves the scene there is usually no strong and well-knit set of lieutenants to carry the organization forward in a coherent way. An abrupt ending of years of dictatorial repression usually leads to an eruption of bitter factions and infighting (think of Yugoslavia after Tito's death).

All right—the contrarian leader follows Rule 1 and delegates almost all decisions to lieutenants. The question then is: which few decisions should he keep for himself?

First, the leader should reserve to himself the hiring, compensating, motivating, molding, assessing and firing of his chief lieutenants. In the long term these may well be the most important decisions that any leader makes (a point that is missed by almost all books on leadership).

Second, the leader himself should make those decisions which have the greatest potential impact on the organization or movement he's leading. Should we sell the company? Should we buy out or merge with a competitor? Should we risk half our net worth on the development of a single new product? Should we close down our medical school? These are questions for the leader, not his lieutenants.

Identifying the really crucial decisions is sometimes referred to as distinguishing between the urgent and the important, which sounds easy in theory but isn't in practice. Here again the news media can be a major stumbling block. The railings of the press can and often do divert the leader's attention away from the really important questions and toward the hot issues of the moment. Just as Ulysses stopped up the ears of his sailors with wax in order to make them immune to the seductive (and destructive) singing of the sirens, so too must the wise leader shield himself from the babble of the media when he's trying to separate the urgent from the important.

Oddly enough, sometimes the most important decisions have to do with apparent trivia. At some point back in the '60s, when public morals were considerably more stringent than they are today, a major flap occurred at a midwestern university over the publication by one of its professors of a "dirty" (i.e., sexually explicit) poem. The president of the university rightly understood that this ostensible tempest-in-a-teapot in fact posed a major threat to both academic freedom and the university's budget. The president therefore chose to invest enormous amounts of his personal time in making all decisions with respect to this controversy. His choice was a good one, since only he had the stature to head off a really catastrophic outcome.

Similarly, when the nation's air traffic controllers engaged in an illegal strike in 1981, President Ronald Reagan, perhaps the most ardent delegator to occupy the White House in the past century, chose to take back to himself much of the authority which he usually delegated to the secretary of transportation. By managing the crisis himself, and personally firing the striking controllers, Reagan guessed correctly that he would greatly strengthen the authority of his presidency in the long run, even though the entire affair was of relatively minor importance in substantive terms.

Machiavelli points out that a leader should never become too predictable, lest his lieutenants and other followers be able to manipulate him too easily. Note the nuance here: it's a healthy thing for a leader to be manipulated to some extent by his followers, and especially by his chief lieutenants; the trick is to keep such manipulation within reasonable limits.

One of the best ways to maintain these limits on predictability and manipulation is for the leader to occasionally make a decision which he would normally delegate to a lieutenant. Doing so throws subordinates off balance just a bit, thereby helping them remember that their authority is delegated to them by the leader, and that consequently they are stewards of something that ultimately belongs to the leader and not to them. An occasional foray of this kind can also greatly improve a lieutenant's sense of accountability and clarify his understanding of the leader's goals and objectives.

For example, it would be counterproductive in most instances for the CEO of a large manufacturing company to inject himself into the details of product design. But by doing so from time to time, he can convey two clear messages: first, that the CEO really cares about the product, and second, that product design must mesh with every other facet of the corporation (as represented by the CEO) if the company is to survive in a competitive market.

Shortly after I became president of USC in March of 1991, I decided to inject myself into the management of our fraternities and sororities. Greek life had a long and noble history at USC, but in recent years had become, shall we say, a bit rowdy and animalistic. I thought a goodly dose of tough love was needed in order to ensure the long-term survival of USC's Greek houses. After asking for and receiving from the students themselves a set of proposed new standards of behavior for Greek organizations, I decided to reject what had been submitted and simply write and promulgate my own rules for what our fraternities and sororities could and should achieve. The short-term result was much wailing and gnashing of teeth; the long-term result has been one of the strongest and finest Greek systems in the country.

Interestingly enough I've never felt the need to inject myself again into the writing of standards for student conduct at USC, perhaps because everyone knows I'm willing to do so if I feel things are going off track and they would all prefer to keep me out of it.

A leader should always be willing to make a decision in order to resolve disputes among his senior lieutenants. Don't let such fights fester; listen carefully to both sides and resolve the issue promptly. If two of your lieutenants are consistently taking up too much of your time with their quarrels, fire one or both of them.

An important factor in choosing which decisions to make is knowing whether or not you really have the authority to make a particular decision. Many aspiring leaders get chewed up by over-reaching the bounds of their jurisdiction—they make brilliant decisions with respect to matters that in fact lie within the domain of some other leader or official, and in the process squander a great deal of their credibility and legitimacy.

George Washington was especially adroit at avoiding this pitfall. Rather than arrogate power to himself, he would often defer to the authority of others (such as a squabbling and incompetent Congress). Only when it was clear to all that the authority to make a certain decision was legitimately his would Washington exercise his power as president. As historian Garry Wills noted in *Certain Trumpets*, "This is the paradox of leadership in a legal system—it asserts authority by deferring to it, as Washington wielded power by giving it up."

In the late 1980s, when I was president of SUNY-Buffalo, our law school faculty decided to ban representatives of the judge advocate general corps from recruiting in the law school building because of the federal government's policy prohibiting homosexuals from serving in the armed forces. The matter was quickly appealed to me. Rather than jump precipitously into the hornet's nest of gays in the military, I decided first to find out who actually had the authority to ban various persons from using a particular university building. Was it the faculty for whom that building was home? The president? The SUNY-Buffalo Governing Council? The chancellor of the SUNY System? The SUNY System Board of Trustees?

Eventually everyone, including even the law school faculty, agreed that the authority to prohibit persons or groups from using university facilities lay exclusively with the president. This process of pinpointing the locus of authority automatically transformed the law faculty's action from an actual *banning* of the JAG corps, to a simple *recommendation* to the president that the JAG corps *should* be banned. This transformation in turn changed the nature of the decision I had to make, because in academic circles it is one thing for a university president to decline to approve a faculty recommendation, and quite another for him to overturn a decision which the faculty feel is legitimately theirs to make.

Moreover, if it had turned out that the authority for banning people from the law school building lay exclusively with the law faculty and not with the president, then I would have been absolved from making any decision at all. I might have publicly expressed agreement or disagreement with the faculty's decision, but I wouldn't have had to take responsibility for it.

The foregoing example is instructive as to why a leader should avoid, whenever possible, engaging in a two-front war when it comes to decision making—that is, quarreling simultaneously over who has the authority to make a particular decision, and what the decision should be.

Presidents John Kennedy, Lyndon Johnson and Richard Nixon were always fighting two battles at once with respect to Vietnam—the actual shooting war in Southeast Asia, and the political war at home over whether the president had the authority to be fighting the North Vietnamese in the first place. As a consequence, Kennedy, Johnson and Nixon were hamstrung at every step of the way, and none of the three was able either to win the war or honorably disengage.

By contrast, President George Bush the elder avoided a two-front war (i.e., one with bullets, the other political) in the Persian Gulf by first laying out the pros and cons of the war for the American people, and then asking Congress to vote on the matter. Had Congress rejected the notion of American intervention, I suppose Bush would have held his nose and allowed Iraq to annex Kuwait. But with Congress and the people behind him, Bush was able to focus all his energies and America's military might on repelling the Iraqi invasion.

Sometimes a leader is well advised to *create* a situation which requires him to make a decision. This technique is especially helpful if the organization of which the leader is in charge has become moribund or indolent, or has lost its focus or *élan vital*.

For example, a new corporate CEO may wish to inform his senior officers that he intends to reduce their number by 30 percent, with the caveat that he will not decide whom to cut until two months hence. Or a university president may announce that it's time for the institution to create a new role and mission statement, and that the president herself will be the principal draftsman for this project. Or the leader of a charity may indicate to his staff that it would be prudent for the organization to drop two of its seven core programs, in order to do a much better job with the remaining five, and that he will decide which two will be dropped after a month's worth of study and consultation. The point is that the impetus for each of these decisions was intentionally created by the leader himself, rather than being thrust upon him by external circumstances.

There is also the need on occasion for a leader to *appear* to be making decisions when in fact he is not. In April of 1992 the city of Los Angeles became engulfed in a horrific and bloody riot, triggered by a jury's acquittal of several police officers who had beaten an arrested motorist named Rodney King. In actual fact the rioters left USC untouched, but at the height of the disturbances (which surrounded the university's campus) we fully expected to suffer widespread arson, looting, beatings, and even murder.

Fortunately the university had a well-developed emergency plan for dealing with a catastrophic *earthquake*. One of our vice presidents, surveying the growing mayhem from the top of a university building during the early hours of the riot, said to himself, "This looks like an earthquake to me!" and forthwith ordered the implementation of our earthquake emergency plan. With that, students from outlying housing were brought in to temporary quarters in the central campus, every university police officer and all physical plant staff were called back to active duty, the perimeter of the campus was secured, observers with radios were placed atop strategic buildings, phone banks were set up to deal with tens of thousands of calls from parents of students and families of staff, and a centralized command-and-control post was opened to coordinate the entire business.

What was the president's role during the three days of rioting? I walked around and showed the flag, so to speak. I shook hands, chatted with students and staff, asked questions, listened to people tell their stories, and gave out copious compliments and reassurances. Everyone thought I was in charge, making seventeen decisions a minute, but I really wasn't. Instead, all the decisions were being made by people who had been trained for months in the handling of a catastrophic emergency.

Was my presence on campus useful? Yes, very. The fact that the president of the university was highly visible night and day during the riots gave everyone a sense of security, which probably helped reduce panic and improve cooperation among our students and staff. But in terms of decision making I followed Rule 1 to the letter: I delegated everything to lieutenants while taking full responsibility for whatever might go wrong.

Finally, when it comes to the question of which decisions he should make and which he should delegate or ignore, the leader is well advised to remember the prayer attributed to Saint Francis of Assisi: "God grant me the serenity to accept the things I cannot change, the courage to change the things I can, and the wisdom to know the difference." As with everything else pertaining to leadership, Saint Francis's advice is not absolute. But the leader who restricts his decision making and associated risk taking to matters that can make a major difference in the long term is probably on the right track.

We now come to the contrarian leader's approach to the timing of decisions, as expressed in Rule 2: never make a decision today that can reasonably be put off till tomorrow. This rule is closely related to thinking gray. And as is the case with suspending judgment about the truth or falsity of incoming information, Rule 2 is so counterintuitive to the average person as to appear ridiculous. But for effective leadership over the long term it is an absolute necessity. I like to call it "artful procrastination."

Almost all sophisticated leaders are artful procrastinators to a greater or lesser extent, but Harry Truman personified this trait. Whenever a staff member would come to him with a problem or opportunity requiring a presidential decision, the first thing Truman would ask was, "How much time do I have?" Was it essential that he make the decision in thirty seconds, in an hour, in a day, sometime next week, in a month, within the year?

Truman well understood that the *timing* of a decision could be as important as the decision itself. A long lead time opened the door for extensive consultation and discussion; a very short lead time meant the president could only look inside his own soul, and then only briefly, for an answer that might affect millions of people.

Truman also knew that he couldn't take his staff member's estimate of the time available at face value. He had to sharply question, and sometimes even bully, a subordinate to learn how much time was *really* available. That's because almost every subordinate who comes to a leader for a decision prefers to have the decision made quickly. There are at least two reasons for this phenomenon. First, a quick decision allows the subordinate to get on with his business and not waste his time waiting around for the leader to make up her mind. This can and should be an important factor in the leader's thinking, but it should never be allowed to *control* the timing of a decision. Second, every subordinate knows that if he comes to the leader with a question and can get a quick decision, the chances are fairly high that the decision will be to the subordinate's liking; after all, the subordinate will probably be the only person whom the leader will consult on the matter.

Queen Elizabeth I is another example of a brilliant leader (at least during the first thirty or so years of her reign) who knew the value of artful procrastination. Perhaps the best example of her skill in this regard was the way in which she played off numerous suitors (and her own senior officials) against each other for two decades over the question of whether and when and whom she should marry.

Elizabeth was under enormous pressure from her government and the English people to marry and produce an heir. She consistently gave the impression that she wanted to marry, intended to marry, and felt the need to marry (e.g., "I am merely a woman, wanting both wit and memory"), but somehow something would always come up that prevented her from *actually getting* married.

For all we know, Elizabeth may never have intended to marry at all, since doing so would almost certainly have reduced her power and perhaps destabilized her realm. But her artful procrastination on this issue worked very much to her own and her country's advantage over a long period of time.

One of the hidden benefits of Rule 2 is that it can open up many more options for the leader than might initially have been available to him. If a decision can be reasonably delayed for, say, a few months, an adversary might die or resign, a competitor might go bankrupt, a court might unexpectedly promulgate an advantageous new "law" (see Chapter 3), or interest rates might decline. To paraphrase the young, "stuff happens," and the stuff that happens is sometimes all to the good.

However, there is also a huge potential downside to Rule 2—namely, waiting too long. Just as procrastination can open up new options for the leader, it can also lead to options being foreclosed. Again, "stuff happens," and the stuff that happens might well be deleterious. So we're back to the question of the timing of decision making, which is an art unto itself.

One of my favorite expressions is "Sometimes no decision by Tuesday is in fact a decision by default." In other words, if failing to make a decision by next Tuesday means that the decision will be effectively removed from the leader's hands by external forces, or that his options will be significantly narrowed, he must have the courage to make a conscious decision by Tuesday and get on with it. For it is one thing for a leader to delegate a decision to a lieutenant, but an entirely different (and unacceptable) thing for him to surrender a decision to fate or to his adversaries. Therein lies the difference between artful and cowardly procrastination.

General George McClellan is a wonderful example of a cowardly procrastinator. Named by Lincoln to command the Army of the Potomac in 1861, McClellan wasted numerous opportunities to seriously engage and perhaps even defeat the Confederate forces. As the historian Garry Wills observed in *Certain Trumpets*, "For McClellan, the doctrine of predominant numbers was a principle of paralysis. He felt he *never* had enough troops, well enough trained or equipped." After McClellan repeatedly squandered the North's military advantage over the South, Lincoln sacked him. McClellan may have simply been the victim of the Peter Principle—a brilliant and talented man promoted just one notch over his head. But certainly his ability to make bold decisions when the time came to make them was almost nil.

Once a contrarian leader has chosen a particular decision to make himself, and knows by what date he must make it, the question remains: *how* should he make it? On what and whom should he rely? Advice from experts and his chief lieutenants? The demands of various constituents (e.g., faculty, students, shareholders, unions, politicians, the media, alumni, neighborhood groups, etc.)? His own judgment and experience? All of the above?

One of my favorite colleagues at SUNY-Buffalo was our CFO, Bob Wagner. Whenever our administrative team would tackle an especially tough decision, Bob would always say, "Remember, in the university, *process* is our most important product!" And to some extent he was right. There's a lot to be said for carefully considering the needs and desires of a broad range of constituents before making a major decision, even if in the end the decision is contrary to what some or all of these constituents would have wanted.

Of course, this kind of consultation is much easier, and may make more sense, in a not-for-profit organization than it does in a profit-seeking company. But even within the for-profit sector, talking with those constituents who will be most affected by a decision prior to actually making it can be very good business.

Over the years I've been privileged to serve on fourteen corporate boards in a wide variety of industries. On occasion I've been amazed at how insensitive some business leaders can be toward their own employees, suppliers, customers and neighbors. Time and again I've watched corporate CEOs and their lieutenants make enemies when they didn't have to, or miss a chance to make important allies at very little cost to the company. This kind of callousness may appear to be in the shareholders' best interests in the short run, but it often turns out to be disastrous for them over the long haul.

It is almost always advantageous, when making a major decision, for the leader to consult with her principal advisers and chief lieutenants. If the decision is a really tough one, the chances are high that the leader's key advisers will be deeply split over the issue. In such cases the leader may have an opportunity to use the decision-making process to build consensus among her inner circle. At the very least the leader may be able to frame the issue so that no lieutenant is left irretrievably humiliated should the final decision be contrary to his advice.

This last point is important, because if a particular lieutenant is on the losing side among the leader's principal advisers too often, he may suddenly be excommunicated by his peers, even though the leader may wish to retain this particular lieutenant as an effective member of her team. Jack London, in *Call of the Wild*, describes how long-running disputes between two sled dogs in the Alaskan wilderness are settled. Eventually the other dogs sit on their haunches in a circle and begin howling while the two antagonists go at each other in the center of the ring. When it's clear that one dog has the upper hand, the other dogs suddenly converge on the loser (i.e., the underdog) and tear him apart. Unfortunately, a leader's cadre of senior lieutenants is sometimes capable of exhibiting this same behavior.

By contrast, it's perfectly acceptable, and sometimes quite salutary, for a leader to go against the unanimous advice of his chief lieutenants. Abraham Lincoln once took a vote among his cabinet on an issue which he himself favored. When he had counted the votes, Lincoln announced, "One aye and seven nays—the ayes have it!" In such cases, the members of the leader's inner circle may grumble a bit about their boss, but they will rarely resort to fomenting a revolution against him for occasionally eschewing their collective advice. (Of course, if the leader is consistently at odds with all his lieutenants, it's time for him either to step down or appoint new lieutenants.)

Another important element in decision-making is chance, or more accurately, probabilities. Machiavelli in *The Prince*, and the great military theorist Karl von Clausewitz in his seminal treatise *On War*, repeatedly make the point that a leader should always take luck and probabilities into careful account when making major decisions. This maxim applies to financial and personnel decisions as well as those relating to warfare.

Thus, in a very real sense, decision-making becomes a game of chance in which the leader is betting against an opponent, or against some set of phenomena (e.g., the weather or the stock

market) over which the leader has no direct control and the behavior of which he cannot predict.

Most would-be leaders are horrified to think of decision-
making as a form of gambling. They much prefer to believe that,
when faced with a difficult decision, the leader should search for
the single best answer (if only it can be discovered) which will
lead with certainty to success. But alas, such amateur leaders
delude themselves. As Machiavelli points out, slightly more than
half of the outcome of any bold undertaking is due to luck.

A close cousin to chance in decision-making is judgment.
Whenever I teach electromagnetic theory to undergraduates in
electrical engineering, I like to tease my students by posing the
following question: At what point should an engineer stop doing
further analysis on a problem and proceed to implement a solution which he knows to be imperfect, and which he knows presents some degree of danger to the public? Most young engineers
(and all tort lawyers) will answer, "Never! Keep searching until
you find the *right* answer, which involves *no* danger to *anyone!*"

But outside the make-believe environment of a courtroom,
such an answer is impracticable if not downright silly. As I point
out to my students, *real* engineers make decisions under a complex set of constraints involving time, cost, size, weight, reliability,
safety, customer appeal, and threats posed by competitors. In short,
real engineers must make *judgments*, which are sometimes based
as much on gut feel as on precise analysis and testing.

One does not need to be a professional engineer to crank out
closed-form analyses of problems that lend themselves to precise
solutions; such work can be done by computers and technicians.
Rather, the exquisite part of engineering involves deciding to
move ahead with a solution based on reasonable professional judgment and analysis, when you know that that solution is not as
good as the one you might develop if you were to keep working
on the problem.

In point of fact, judgment is often the key element of effective leadership in a broad range of human endeavors. Of course,

judgment should always be informed by fact and analysis. But the contrarian leader knows that, in most decision-making situations, the facts and analyses available to him are at best incomplete, and at worst out-and-out wrong. Thus, in the end he must often rely on his own good judgment and that of his advisers.

In most instances, the gathering of factual information and the carrying out of analyses on which a leader will base his decisions are done by subordinates who are pretty low on the totem pole. Just as a leader should occasionally reach down and make a decision which he would normally delegate to a lieutenant, so should the leader occasionally go down into the trenches and gather some information or supervise a particular analysis first-hand. I call this "counting the widgets in the stockroom yourself." It's amazing how often you'll find that the allegedly factual information you've been receiving for years about a particular matter is completely erroneous, not because the person gathering the information is malicious or incompetent, but simply because he misunderstood what it was he was supposed to count or misinterpreted how he was supposed to count it.

The English economist Sir Josiah Stamp once quoted a judge who observed: "The government are very keen on amassing statistics. They collect them, add them, raise them to the nth power, take the cube root and prepare wonderful diagrams. But you must never forget that every one of these figures comes in the first instance from the village watchman who just puts down what he damn pleases."

This concept of occasionally counting the widgets yourself can also be applied to the interpretation of laws and regulations. As was pointed out in Chapter 3, it can be very helpful for the leader and his chief lieutenants to read for themselves the actual statutes and court decisions that apply to a particular situation. An increasingly important feature of the American legal system is its unpredictability and lack of clarity; thus, a firsthand knowledge of the actual written law can be helpful to a leader and his principal advisers as they weigh probabilities and formulate strategies.

Another contrarian discipline with respect to decision-making is to completely ignore any so-called sunk costs—i.e., costs incurred (or mistakes committed) in the past. Decisions made by a leader can only influence the future, not the past. What's done is done and cannot be undone, so the leader must steel himself to only look forward in time, even when there are enormous emotional factors encouraging him to try to justify his past losses and earlier errors in judgment.

How often have we heard the sad story of a compulsive gambler who feels he must continue to bet in order to "win back his losses"? Rationally, a person's past losses at a gaming table should never be an encouragement for him to continue betting; indeed, quite the opposite. But conventional human behavior in this regard tends to be highly irrational.

Those of us who are not compulsive gamblers may smile patronizingly at the foregoing example. But consider the CEO who has spent $100 million of his company's capital to acquire an asset which has proven to be very unprofitable, and who now has an opportunity to sell this asset to someone else for $25 million. Rationally this CEO should sell, unless he genuinely believes the asset is worth more than $25 million or will soon appreciate in value. But time and again, CEOs in this position have retained the bad asset in order to avoid having to admit to themselves (and to their boards and shareholders) that their initial investment was a mistake. And more often than not, the asset in question continues to depreciate in value.

This same foolish tendency to permit sunk costs to influence a leader's decisions can manifest itself in many other ways—from his being unwilling to dismiss a subordinate whom he appointed and who is clearly not working out, to his continuing to attack an enemy's impregnable position after he has squandered several thousand troops in the attempt.

Thinking gray is difficult, and thinking free is even more so, but ignoring sunk costs is the most difficult of all. And yet that is exactly what the contrarian leader knows he must do if he is to make the best possible decision in a given situation.

Finally, when making really important decisions, a contrarian leader listens carefully to his conscience or, if he is religious, to his God. The operative word here is *listens*. When most people try to carry on a conversation with their inner voice (be it the voice of God or conscience), they wind up doing all the talking. That's because we naturally fear our inner voice—we're afraid it might tell us something we don't want to hear. Nonetheless, listening carefully to that voice for twenty minutes or so through contemplative prayer or silent meditation is often a key factor in making good decisions in the long run.

Decision making brings together many of the finest traits of contrarian leadership—thinking gray, thinking free, artful listening, delegating authority while retaining ultimate responsibility, artful procrastination, ignoring sunk costs, taking luck into account, and listening to one's inner voice. Weaving these traits together is an art in itself. When it is done well, the result is a thing of beauty and a powerful tool for effective leadership.

[Handwritten notes:]
thinking grey
thinking free
artful listening
delegating authority while retaining ultimate resp.
artful procrastination
ignoring sunk costs
taking luck into acct.
listen to inner voice

Chapter 6

Give the Devil His Due

Stretch your imagination for a moment. A contrarian leader is at a cocktail party attended by famous figures from throughout the ages. Over the course of the evening, Plato, Mother Theresa and Niccolò Machiavelli all discreetly slip him copies of their résumés, each one greatly interested in serving as his chief adviser. By now you may have guessed what the contrarian leader would do: he would think gray about the matter for as long as he could, perhaps read a supertext or two for inspiration, and then pick up the phone and say, "Mr. Machiavelli, I want *you* to be on my team."

Of course, you may be thinking to yourself that it's one thing to be a contrarian, but it's quite another to argue that old Uncle Niccolò would make a better adviser than history's greatest philosopher or the most beloved humanitarian of recent times. But it is precisely my goal in this chapter to convince you otherwise.

Plato, who in this scenario receives only a polite letter of acknowledgment for his interest in the job, once made the following statement about leadership: "Until philosophers are kings, or the kings and princes of this world have the spirit and power of philosophy, and political greatness and wisdom meet in one, and those commoner natures who pursue either to the exclusion of the other are compelled to stand aside, cities will never have rest from their evils." Heady stuff. Yet, almost as though he were responding directly to Plato, Machiavelli soberly observed some two thousand years later that:

> Many have imagined republics and principalities which have never been seen or known to exist in reality; for how we live is so far removed from how we ought to live, that he who abandons what is done for what ought to be done will rather bring about his own ruin than his preservation; for a man who strives after goodness in all his acts is sure to come to ruin, since there are so many who are not good. Hence it is necessary that a prince who is interested in his survival learn to be other than good, making use of this capacity or refraining from it according to the need.

As the historian Bernard Crick noted, "Machiavelli was a sword which was plunged into the flank of the body politic of Western humanity, causing itself to cry out and struggle with itself. The pain is still with us, and if we ever cease to feel that pain, it will not be because the conditions that gave rise to it have miraculously vanished, but rather because our nerves have gone dead."

For better or worse, Niccolò Machiavelli is the father of modern political science and is still a very powerful force to be reckoned with. Let's add some perspective. We noted in Chapter 4 that there are only a few texts which are four hundred years old or more and which are still widely read today. These supertexts include the Judeo-Christian Bible, the Qur'an, the Bhagavad Gita, the plays of Shakespeare, Plato's *Republic*, Machiavelli's *Prince*, and a handful of others. Of these supertexts, only *The Prince* could be considered to be primarily a manual on leadership.

Moreover, *The Prince* is quite probably the most misunderstood supertext of all. And because such an influential book has been so misunderstood through the ages, it's important to be familiar with the basis for this misunderstanding and its ramifications for how we lead people and organizations.

Let's begin with a bit of historical background. Niccolò Machiavelli (1469–1527) lived in the middle of the Italian Renaissance, a period that witnessed great changes in politics, religion, technology, exploration and war. He came from a prominent Florentine family, but his own father was not wealthy; as a consequence Niccolò was denied a university education, which some scholars believe is the reason he was able to write so clearly and compellingly.

Machiavelli served in a number of important political posts in the Florentine republic until 1512, when the pope's army reinstated the Medici family as the rulers of Florence. Suspected of having played a part in a conspiracy to overthrow the new government, Machiavelli was tortured and, some scholars say, beaten nearly to death. He steadfastly maintained his innocence, however, and was eventually allowed to return to his family farm, where he wrote *The Prince* and other works.

Machiavelli actually presented *The Prince* as a gift to the man whose minions had tortured him, Lorenzo de' Medici, in a vain attempt to win an appointment in the Florentine government. Finally, after Lorenzo died, Machiavelli was appointed to a number of minor bureaucratic and academic posts which sustained him for the rest of his life.

Not long after his death, Machiavelli's name became synonymous with deceit, cynicism and evil machinations, and it has retained that negative connotation to this day. But in actual fact, Machiavelli himself was an honorable man and a loyal patriot who was devoted to his family. So why the disconnect? Why should a man of principle be so widely reviled, and yet at the same time so widely read and quoted?

When reading *The Prince*, one must remember that Machiavelli is writing, not for leaders in general, but for a very special kind of leader which he labels with the Italian word *principe*. We translate Machiavelli's term with the English word *prince*, but the two are really quite different.

In Machiavelli's lexicon, a principe is the leader of a sovereign state who must compete with other principi in a world in which there are no overarching laws or rules. Depending on the type of office he holds (absolute monarch, elected head of a republic, etc.), a principe may or may not be constrained by law and custom when it comes to internal affairs. But in external affairs there are no constraints; each principe and the sovereign state he leads are engaged in a no-holds-barred competition with all other sovereign states.

That's the point that most people miss when reading *The Prince*. Machiavelli's analysis and advice are not always applicable to a leader who operates in an arena in which everyone, including the leader and his competitors, is subject to laws imposed by a higher power.

Thus, for example, Machiavelli would advise a principe who has recently gained control of a particular principality to quickly extinguish the line of the former leader of that principality, which is a euphemism for murdering the deposed principe and his children and grandchildren. This would decidedly not be good advice for a modern CEO who successfully acquires a competitor through a hostile takeover.

On the other hand, Machiavelli's advice that, if forced to make an exclusive choice between the two, a principe should prefer to be feared rather than loved by his subjects, and above all not be hated by them, may be very good advice for a modern business leader.

Let's consider a truly barbaric scenario. A country is locked in a fierce and ruthless war with another nation. The war was initiated through an unprovoked attack on the first country by the second. In a shocking act of retaliation, the emperor of the nation that was attacked sentences thousands of the aggressor nation's women and children to be burned to death. This action weakens the resolve of the aggressor and helps lead ultimately to its unconditional surrender. The emperor who ordered the deaths of the enemy's civilians is then celebrated as a hero by his subjects. Objectively, though, can he be seen as anything other than a villain willing to turn innocent women and children into mere pawns on the chessboard of war? But that's exactly the manner of action that was taken by President Harry Truman—a hero to me and to many others—when he authorized the incendiary bombings of Tokyo. Roughly a million people were reportedly killed, most of them women and children who were burned alive. And this was before the horrors of Hiroshima and Nagasaki.

Machiavelli would have seen all these events in a somewhat different light, having acknowledged that, for a principe to do the greatest good, he must occasionally be willing to do bad. In other words, principi must learn to live with dirt on their hands in order to achieve larger ends. In the foregoing example, Truman sincerely (and perhaps correctly) believed it was necessary to carry out certain horrible retaliatory acts in order to minimize overall suffering and loss of life in bringing about the total defeat of Japan.

Do the terrible wartime choices of the head of a sovereign nation, ancient or contemporary, even remotely compare to the choices that must be made by the leader of a typical twenty-first-century organization? Yes, sometimes.

At the level of a sovereign nation the challenges that arise may require war and bloodshed. At the level of a corporation the challenges may require downsizing or takeovers. And at the level of an individual leader the challenges may require laying off a good friend or a worker whose family needs medical benefits. Some leadership gurus argue that the most benevolent approach to these challenges in the short run will prevent the worst outcomes in the long run, but history has rarely shown this to be the case. With that in mind, there's a great deal we can learn from Machiavelli, especially after we clear away a few of the myths and misconceptions about his advice.

Let me clarify the most fundamental misunderstanding. Machiavelli was not an immoral or even an amoral man; as mentioned earlier, he had a strong set of moral principles. But he was driven by the notion of a *higher* good: an orderly state in which citizens can move about at will, conduct business, safeguard their families and possessions, and be free of foreign intervention or domination. Anything which could harm this higher good, Machiavelli argued, must be opposed vigorously and ruthlessly. Failure to do so out of either weakness or kindness was condemned by Machiavelli as being contrary to the interests of the state, just as it would be contrary to the interests of a patient for his surgeon to refuse to perform a needed operation out of fear that doing so would inflict pain on the patient.

Does the foregoing sound like a thinly veiled apologia for the old (and, most of us would say, repugnant) idea that the end justifies the means? Yes, it is exactly that. Gad! How can a university president in the twenty-first century even hint that he approves of such a noxious notion? The answer is, I don't. But Machiavelli would argue that all people believe, to a greater or lesser extent, that *under certain circumstances* the end justifies the means. And as with all things Machiavellian, the key point is not what *should* be so but what *is* so in fact.

Machiavelli's primary contribution was not a static set of leadership principles, but rather his painfully honest observations about human nature. He observed (correctly, I might say) that a technique which works at one time and place may not work in another. A good leader recognizes this fact and, using history as his guide, adapts to the demands of the moment.

I certainly don't agree with all of what Machiavelli had to say, but I find much of it illuminating and provocative. Among his more cogent and controversial points are:

- No policy is without its peril. A really talented leader first discerns the pitfalls of each option and then chooses the

best among them, recognizing that there is no perfect or perfectly popular solution.

- The preservation of civil unity and the prevention of foreign
intervention or domination are sufficient to justify almost
any action by a principe.

- Men must either be cajoled or be crushed, for if you do a
person a slight injury he will surely avenge himself, but if
you crush him he cannot.

- No principe should submit to evil in order to avoid a war
(think of Neville Chamberlain's failure to confront Hitler
prior to World War II).

- Fortune (i.e., luck) plays the greatest role in determining the
success of any leader, and fortune favors the bold. Fortune
can be more easily mastered by the rash and the violent
than by those who proceed more slowly and coldly.

- It may be acceptable to kill the male leaders of a conquered
nation, but the conquering principe should ensure that his
army leaves the citizens' property and their women undis-
turbed.

- In a newly conquered territory, the leader should implement his
harshest acts all at once, but string out benefits and mercies, so
that the people might come to appreciate him over time.

- The major responsibilities of a good principe include: being
a lover of virtue (faking it, if necessary); encouraging the
vocations and talents of the citizenry; letting men keep their
possessions and their women; maintaining incorruptible and
ethical ministers and judges; and, above all, defending the
principality from foreign domination.

As noted, Machiavelli believed that it is all right for a leader to
be either loved or feared but not hated. And if he must choose
between the first two, it is better to be feared than loved.

The dictator Joseph Stalin personified this principle. Despite his having been responsible for the deaths of millions of citizens of the Soviet Union, the general populace never hated him. They certainly *feared* him, and indeed this very fear caused many Soviet citizens to develop a sort of perverted affection for the old butcher. Even Americans such as Eisenhower and Truman found Stalin worthy of a certain respect and admiration.

Of course, a principal reason for Stalin's ability to avoid being hated by his followers was his ability to control the press. At the beginning of the twenty-first century, the Internet, cellular telephony and other technologies have made it far more difficult for dictators and despots to avoid earning the contempt of their followers—another reason for democracy's global success.

So Machiavelli's advice is not simply that a leader should be feared by his followers. Indeed, he would say that the best course for any leader is to be feared and loved at the same time. But Machiavelli would go on to say that, if it is impossible to be both—that is, if the leader is forced for whatever reason to make an exclusive choice between the two—then he should always choose fear over love. The reason Machiavelli gives is simple: people are more likely to take advantage of a leader who is only loved than they are one who is feared:

> Men have less hesitation in offending one who makes himself beloved than one who makes himself feared; for love holds by a bond of obligation which, as mankind is bad, is broken on every occasion whenever it is for the interest of the obliged party to break it. But fear holds by the apprehension of punishment, which never leaves men.

He gives both a positive and a negative example of this principle, the former being the Carthaginian general Hannibal (247–183 B.C.):

> Among the many admirable qualities of Hannibal, it is related of him that, having an immense army composed of a very great variety of races and men, which he led to war in

foreign countries, no quarrels ever occurred among them, nor were there any dissensions between them and their chief, either in his good or in his adverse fortunes; which can only be accounted for by his extreme cruelty. This, together with his boundless courage, made him ever venerated and terrible in the eyes of his soldiers; and without that extreme severity all his other virtues would not have sufficed to produce that result.

And the latter being the Roman general Scipio (237–183 B.C.):

Scipio's armies revolted in Spain solely in consequence of his extreme clemency, which allowed his soldiers more license than comports with proper military discipline. This fact was censured in the Roman Senate by Fabius Maximus, who called Scipio the corrupter of the Roman soldiers.

Here again it is important to remember that *The Prince* is a handbook for principi, not Boy Scout leaders. Nonetheless, effective leadership at any level, from parenting to running a large corporation, requires that the leader lay down rules and evenhandedly punish those who break the rules. While it may seem counterintuitive to those of us raised in an era of warm and fuzzy feelings, evenhanded but brutal justice on the part of a leader can give rise to a sense of security and warmth among his followers. I am certainly not recommending that a leader should engage in brutality, nor am I suggesting that he should eschew mercy. But the failure of a leader to enforce the rules out of a desire to incur the affection of his followers can bring that leader to ruin in a hurry.

A related lesson taught by Machiavelli is: Don't humiliate an opponent unless you're sure you are able, and want, to eliminate him altogether. Otherwise you'll simply make an enemy for life.

Machiavelli pointed out that there is no quicker way to incur the permanent hatred of a defeated people than for the conqueror to take their property or desecrate their women. If a principe wins a new state he can probably kill off some or all of the ruling class, because the chances are the general populace won't have loved the prior ruling class all that much anyway. And the new principe might even levy new taxes without incurring the enmity of the people. But if he seizes the people's property outright or violates their women, they will hate him *forever*.

All the bad press Machiavelli has received notwithstanding, we should give him credit for being a man of practical virtue. Many leaders over the last five hundred years may have imagined that they are far more scrupulous than the old Italian, but in the end some of these leaders violated one of Machiavelli's basic tenets by subjecting defeated adversaries to the kind of humiliation that breeds hatred of, and ultimately disaster for, the leader.

A story about Douglas MacArthur, who was apparently something of a student of Machiavelli, is apropos here, even though it may be apocryphal. After the unconditional surrender of Japan at the conclusion of World War II, MacArthur was installed by the Allies as the absolute ruler of that country. He quickly issued an order that forbade, on pain of death, the raping of Japanese women by American soldiers. When a small number of GIs were caught defying MacArthur's order, they were arrested and court-martialed, and those who were convicted were sentenced to death. MacArthur then invited a group of senior Japanese officials to witness the executions. This had a stunning effect on the Japanese leadership. It was inconceivable to them that a conquering general would execute his own men for simply raping the women of a conquered people; after all, rape has been a conqueror's right for millennia. But MacArthur followed Machiavelli's contrarian advice instead of historical precedent, and as a consequence he obtained the total cooperation of the Japanese people in discharging his duties as dictator.

By contrast, age-old conflicts involving Serbs, Croatians, Bosnians, Turks, Armenians, Chinese, Japanese and Koreans all reveal that, wherever the wholesale desecration of women has taken place, there is often a bitter desire for payback that can last for decades or centuries. There is no limit in time or intensity to the hatred that the raping of a defeated nation's women can engender.

The vast majority of leaders will never play at the level of a MacArthur or a Milosevic, but Machiavelli's advice applies just as well in far more mundane circumstances. Over the course of a successful leader's career he will "defeat" many other people, perhaps by buying out another company, firing a cantankerous subordinate, or leapfrogging over a set of rivals. If the leader insists that the defeated persons also be humiliated, whether out of spite or recklessness, the vanquished will not rest until they have found a way to avenge themselves.

During my tenure as president of SUNY-Buffalo, I came to learn that its transformation from a private university to a public university in 1962 involved a senseless humiliation that hurt the university for years thereafter. At the time, Governor Nelson Rockefeller was trying to establish a public university system for New York—the only state in the union that still lacked one. The state already owned several small teachers' colleges, two freestanding medical schools, and an assortment of specialized professional schools. Rockefeller cobbled these disparate units together to form the State University of New York.

However, he still needed a flagship campus. He and his minions quickly settled on the idea of acquiring the private University at Buffalo (which at that time was struggling for survival) and transforming it into SUNY's flagship. Its financial difficulties notwithstanding, UB (as it was known) was governed by a board of trustees made up of proud men and women who had invested dearly in the institution. These trustees were basically in favor of UB's being acquired by SUNY, but they had a few minor concerns which they wanted to negotiate.

But Governor Rockefeller, in his inimitably arrogant style, made it clear there would be no negotiations. Either the UB trustees would accept the terms dictated by the state, or a nearby teachers' college would be turned into a comprehensive SUNY campus, thereby ensuring UB's demise. The trustees of UB considered the matter and capitulated. But the governor hadn't left them with their shorts on. When I arrived at UB two decades later to serve as president, many people associated with the university still despised and reviled the state. Rockefeller had humiliated the UB trustees over peanuts, and they and their friends still hated him and his bureaucracy long after he was dead.

That's Machiavelli's point. A leader can impose a wide range of harsh strictures on his followers and not be hated by them, even when those whom he is leading are not his followers by choice. But if he humiliates them in addition to dealing harshly with them, they and their successors will never forgive him.

Niccolò Machiavelli was above all a student of human nature. His repeated advice to leaders was to believe in the *reality* of human nature, as opposed to what they *wished* it were.

I am reminded here of a book on child rearing by Dr. Hiam Ginott which my wife and I read many years ago. Dr. Ginott advised parents to teach their children the supreme importance of discerning and accepting reality, in order either to make peace with it or to attempt to change it. In other words, don't let children delude themselves about how the world and its people really work. That's exactly what Machiavelli was trying to do for adults. We must accept the fact that human beings and their institutions hardly ever measure up to our noblest ideals, and that to pretend otherwise is to invite ruin.

Admittedly, Machiavelli had an especially negative and cynical view of human nature. That view might well have been justified in sixteenth-century Florence, especially for a man who had been brutally tortured and denigrated by the government of a city which he had served with loyalty and distinction.

A somewhat more balanced view of human nature is presented in Table 1. Here I have listed, in alphabetical order, some eighty-two traits or aspects, most of which I suspect have been

TABLE 1. A Few More or Less Universal Aspects of Human Nature.

adornment	goals	punishment
agreements	greed	rape
altruism	grudges	religion
ambition	guilt	revenge
anger	happiness	ritual
apology	hate	sacrifice
art	hierarchy	sadness
betrayal .	history	secrets
bullying	imagination	shame
causality	invention	slavery
competition	jealousy	stargazing
confession	killing	storytelling
conscience	kindness	suspicion
conspiracy	language	sympathy
cooperation	laughter	taboos
counting	law	teaching
deceitfulness	leadership	technology
dissatisfaction	love	theft
distrust	loyalty	tools
embarrassment	lying	torture
enemies	marriage	tradition
enthusiasm	mercy	tribalism
explanation	names	trust
exploration	ownership	war
family	pillaging	weapons
forgiveness	planning	wondering
friendship	polygamy	
gender	pride	

exhibited from time to time by various individuals in every human society that has existed over the past hundred thousand years. Moreover, I suspect that every human being who has ever lived, or ever will live, is capable of exhibiting nearly every one of these traits or aspects under the right set of circumstances.

For example, when I was president of SUNY-Buffalo I made several visits to China prior to the 1989 Tiananmen Square demonstrations and massacre. During all of these visits the Chinese people proved to be exceptionally honest. You could lose your wallet on the street and it would be returned; you could leave your hotel room unlocked and nothing would be taken. But our SUNY-Buffalo staff who were quartered in Beijing reported that as soon as the Tiananmen Square killings began, Beijing returned almost instantly to its traditional practices of bribery and extortion.

Similarly, when rioting broke out in Los Angeles in April of 1992 as a result of the Rodney King case, we saw everyday citizens looting stores, torching buildings and beating passersby.

But one of the most striking illustrations of the dark potential of ordinary human beings came to light some three decades ago, when Stanford University psychologists selected twenty-one healthy and normal local citizens who were willing to "staff" a mock prison. Roughly half of these volunteers were randomly tapped to serve as prison guards, and the others were tapped to serve as prisoners. Within hours, the guards—most of whom were normally nonconfrontational—launched into brutal authoritarian displays, and many of the prisoners soon grew depressed, anxious or downright rebellious. The experiment, which was to have lasted two weeks, was suspended after less than one week. Once again, a relatively modest change in circumstances (in this case, even a change which the participants knew to be fictitious) brought about dramatic changes in character.

Of course, we could also recount numerous examples from real life in which humans have been moved to exhibit altruistic and uplifting characteristics under difficult or degrading circumstances. The point is, most people are capable of exhibiting nearly every characteristic listed in Table 1. In that sense, these eighty-two aspects or characteristics suggest the broad range of human potentialities.

Machiavelli wasn't totally right or totally wrong. He showed us a side of human nature which, painful as it may be, every leader must come to grips with. The good news is that there are other facets of human nature that have just as much chance of coming to the fore as those identified by Machiavelli.

Sure, it's natural for people to lie, pillage, hate, seek revenge, make war, and torture prisoners. But it's also natural for people to love, cooperate, have friends, exhibit sympathy, obey the law, and create beautiful works of art. The challenge for the leader isn't to delude himself into thinking that people are intrinsically better or worse than they really are; rather, it is to find ways to bring out the best in his followers (and in himself) while minimizing the worst.

Chapter 7

Know Which Hill
You're Willing to Die On

Most people confuse *good* leadership with *effective* leadership, but the contrarian leader knows that there is an enormous difference between the two. Hitler, for example, was an extraordinarily effective leader (at least during his rise to power and for the first decade or so of his reign), but few would call him a good leader; indeed, most of us would say he was a monstrously evil one.

It's relatively easy for people to agree on the characteristics of an effective leader: he has a clear and compelling vision; inspires trust, commitment and self-sacrifice among his followers; chooses capable lieutenants; keeps his eye on the goal; and pushes himself and others relentlessly. But it is impossible to assess whether a leader is good or bad without recourse to moral values, and most particularly to the moral values of the person making the assessment. Thus the goodness of a leader, as opposed to his effectiveness, is very much in the eye of the beholder.

When I turned sixteen it was finally my turn to take control of the wheel of a car, but not before my father gave me a stern lecture. "If a cat or dog or squirrel runs in front of your car," he told me, "just steel yourself and kill it like a man. You have an obligation not to endanger people in your car or in other cars by swerving in an effort to save an animal." Tough advice, especially for a young man who loved animals as much as I did (and still do).

Have you ever tried to do what my dad suggested? It's really very difficult. But whether I agreed with him or not, I knew Dad was trying to convey to me one of his cherished moral principles— that people are intrinsically more important than animals.

Now let's raise the ante a bit with a question from an old army ethics test. You're a soldier driving a bus down a narrow mountain road, with a wall of granite on one side and a two-hundred-foot drop-off on the other. As you round a corner, a five-year-old girl suddenly dashes out into the middle of the road to retrieve her ball. There's time to do only one of three things: stay on course and kill the girl; or intentionally swerve and kill yourself by falling over the drop-off; or hit the brakes, skid, and swerve, thereby killing both yourself *and* the girl. Most of the army recruits who took this test said they'd go over the drop-off to avoid hitting the little girl, even though the situation was in some sense the girl's fault.

The recruits were then asked to consider the same scenario, but with nineteen other soldiers in the bus with the driver. Here the obvious ethical choice is to stay on course and intentionally kill the little girl. But how many of us could bring ourselves to actually do such a thing? It's hard enough to follow my dad's advice and intentionally run over a dog; think how much harder it would be to steel oneself and intentionally kill a child, even though in this case there's a 20-to-1 gain in lives saved by doing so.

The question can be made even tougher by adding a few variations—e.g., you are alone in the bus but you're carrying information which is crucial to your battalion's success in a battle soon to be waged. Or you are alone in the bus and the girl is "merely" a child of the enemy, and thus not nearly as valuable as even one able-bodied soldier in your own country's army.

These questions are so tough, so painful, that most people simply refuse to address them at all. They can't bring themselves to face up to really difficult moral choices. But doing so is the essence of good leadership, and often of effective leadership as well.

I call this kind of moral choosing "deciding which hill you're willing to die on." And just as Thoreau correctly observed that reading one book necessarily precludes our reading a hundred others, so it is that making one set of moral choices precludes our making many others. If I'm really willing to die on *this* hill, then I'm probably willing to retreat from all the surrounding hills.

Triage in a war zone is a helpful image here. A doctor at a military field hospital sorts through the wounded, recognizing that some will get better with a little attention at a later time, others must be operated on right away in order to save their lives, and still others are irretrievably lost and must be set aside to die. Make no mistake, that doctor is making tough and complex moral judgments, and he would be shirking his duty if he were unwilling or unable to make those judgments and take responsibility for them. So it is with leaders.

Discussions of historical leadership from a moral perspective usually involve a black-and-white approach, with Washington and Gandhi at one extreme and Hitler and Attila the Hun at the other. Yet in actuality, most of humanity's major leaders have had their good points and their bad, just like the rest of us.

Abraham Lincoln was a wildly controversial figure in his own day, trying to balance moral considerations with practical ones—rarely to the satisfaction of anyone. In a terrible irony, John F. Kennedy once reportedly remarked that Lincoln wouldn't have been remembered nearly so fondly had he not made that fateful trip to Ford's Theater.

Though they were contemporaries, and both were significant political figures, no one ever confused Niccolò Machiavelli with Thomas More (1474–1535), the great martyr of the Catholic Church who stood up to King Henry VIII. Most commentators give horns to Machiavelli and a halo to More, but I think that's too simplistic. I would argue that the tendency to caricature these two men is precisely what prevents people from understanding what it is that distinguishes truly exceptional leaders from common ones.

Sir Thomas More (more recently Saint Thomas More) enjoys an idealized image that could hardly be improved upon. Samuel Johnson described Sir Thomas as "the person of the greatest virtue these islands ever produced." That is certainly in keeping with the common image of the man. However, I prefer the more nuanced and complex picture painted by Robert Bolt in his outstanding play, *A Man for All Seasons*. In the introduction to his play, Bolt says:

> Thomas More, as I wrote about him, became for me a man with an adamantine sense of his own self. He knew where he began and left off, what area of himself he could yield to the encroachment of his enemies, and what to the encroachments of those he loved. It was a substantial area in both cases, for he had a proper sense of fear and was a busy lover. Since he was a clever man and a great lawyer, he was able to retire from those areas in wonderfully good order, but at length he was asked to retreat from that final area where he located his self. And there this supple, humorous, unassuming and sophisticated person set like metal, was overtaken by an absolutely primitive rigor, and could no more be budged than a cliff.

More, the author of *Utopia* and lord chancellor for Henry VIII, enjoyed a sweep of power in his time that was second only to the king's. He cheerfully condemned dozens of heretics to be burned at the stake, and maintained a secret police network that would have been the envy of the KGB. Yet he walked away from it all when Henry broke England's ties with the Church of Rome in order to divorce his wife Catherine and marry Anne Boleyn.

That's where the caricature of More begins to take shape. Whereas Machiavelli is usually (and erroneously) depicted as being completely unprincipled, More is viewed as being uncompromisingly resolute in living out his convictions. Yet, as Robert Bolt points out, this is only a cartoon of the real man.

More was a complicated leader who had a genuine desire to serve his friend the king, to care for his family, and to make peace with those matters he couldn't control. More wasn't willing to openly support Henry's intended divorce from Catherine, but he didn't immediately step down over the matter. When Henry first established the Church of England, More decided that would not be a hill worth dying on and chose to continue to fulfill his official duties. But when England's bishops yielded power to Henry and the English church broke its ties with Rome, More walked way from his position as lord chancellor. Even this he did quietly—not as an angry man thundering denunciations against the regime, but as a man who chose to withdraw from public life, without rancor or fanfare. He still hadn't found the hill on which he was willing to die.

More hoped his silence would be interpreted as an act of loyalty to the king, not as dissent. But his hope was in vain. Unwilling to take an oath acknowledging the legitimacy of Henry's divorce and the king's authority in religious matters, More was eventually convicted of high treason (on perjured testimony) and beheaded. Here is how Bolt describes the events that ultimately led to More's martyrdom:

> If, on any day up to that of his execution, he had been willing to give public approval to Henry's marriage with Anne Boleyn, he could have gone on living. Of course the marriage was associated with other things—the attack on the abbeys, the whole Reformation policy—to which More was violently opposed, but I think he could have found his way round those; he showed every sign of doing so. Unfortunately his approval of the marriage was asked for in a form that required him to state that he believed what he didn't believe, and required him to state it in an oath.

That, then, was the hill More was finally willing to die on.

The life and death of a person such as Thomas More raise some of the most important questions that a leader must ask himself: How much ground can I yield and still be true to my moral core? How far can I be pushed before I will need to walk away from my duties? Are there some battles that I should be willing to lose in order to try to win other more important victories for the organization or cause or group that I am leading? What is the particular hill (if any) from which I will never retreat, and in defense of which I am willing, if necessary, to sacrifice everything?

Now here's one of the most contrarian bits of advice you can imagine: Once you know which hill you're really willing to die on, *keep it to yourself*. If you as a leader reveal to everyone the areas of moral behavior on which you are absolutely unwilling to compromise under any circumstances, your adversaries will almost surely use this knowledge to ensnare or undermine you.

Most of us would be inclined to dismiss the foregoing advice as reprehensible or worse. But in the *realpolitik* of serious leadership, a bit of discretion about one's inner self is always the better part of valor (think of poor Coriolanus in Shakespeare's play by that name). It's fine to reveal, or even trumpet, your core values, but be careful about telling the world the exact location of the hill you're willing to die on.

When considering the concept of moral leadership, one must first recognize that there is a significant difference between *legal* behavior on the one hand and *ethical* behavior on the other. Granted, a leader who breaks the laws of the land with impunity will not generally be considered a moral leader; but there's more to it than simply observing the laws.

For instance, it's perfectly legal to urge young adults to take up smoking, or to make promises in a political campaign that you have no intention of keeping, or to cheat on your spouse and have all manner of extramarital relationships, or to take advantage of the weak and vulnerable in your business dealings, but I don't think any of the foregoing actions are ethical. Conversely, in my judgment it is perfectly ethical to break into a cabin in the woods in the middle of a snowstorm in order to save your own or others' lives, or for a black seamstress to refuse to give up her seat in the whites-only section of a bus that is segregated by law, or to use excessive force in defending yourself against a violent attack by hoodlums, even though none of the foregoing actions is legal. The point is, the law provides very little guidance as to what is or is not ethical behavior, especially for leaders.

One popular definition of moral or ethical behavior is that it's what you're willing to do on others' behalf when no one is there to check up on you or force you to do it. With this definition in mind, it's interesting to ask people the source of their moral values. Most respond by referring to their religion, and indeed it would seem that much of what we call moral or altruistic behavior does in fact derive from religious beliefs. As Francis Bacon said in the seventeenth century, "All good moral philosophy is but the handmaiden to religion."

Of course, there are strong (and occasionally convincing) arguments which attempt to explain certain kinds of altruistic behavior in terms of natural selection. Almost everyone would agree, for example, that it makes evolutionary sense for a mother to sacrifice herself in defense of her offspring, or even, perhaps, for a man to sacrifice himself for the good of his hunting group.

But it's a bit of a stretch to explain really breathtaking examples of altruism and moral restraint in purely biological terms. In most such cases the persons performing great feats of self-sacrifice have been motivated by spiritual beliefs that transcend the cold impersonality of a completely mechanistic world.

Indeed, I've concluded that essentially no one *really* believes in mechanistic determinism, even though many people throughout history have claimed to do so. In reality, every human believes in his own free will—that is, in his ability to choose to do or not do various things independently of prior events. Most of us also ascribe this same freedom of choice (and concomitant responsibility) to others.

For example, who among us could watch a beloved family member being beaten to death for sport without holding those doing the beating responsible for their actions? A true believer in mechanistic determinism would shrug his shoulders and say that every phenomenon in the universe is a predetermined and inevitable consequence of past events, and therefore those doing the beating are no more responsible for their actions than an apple is responsible for falling from its tree. But when it comes to real people in real life, mechanistic determinism is simply philosophical nonsense.

In order for a leader to know which hill he's willing to die on—to know where his adamantine core is located—he needs to be consciously aware of his own moral beliefs and what the basis is for those beliefs. If not religious (or at least transcendental) in origin, one's core moral values may prove very unreliable in a clutch, especially if they are in some sense altruistic.

Many people today give lip service to the late-eighteenth-century utilitarian view that each person should place the highest value on the happiness of the greatest number of people. Yet that notion is not nearly as rational as the idea that each person should look out purely for his own interests (which might include the interests of his family or his hunting group) and let Mother Nature sort out the rest; indeed, the latter proposition increasingly appears to have the unequivocal support of evolutionary biology and Mother Nature herself. Mao, Mussolini, Stalin and various other despots have shown that a nonaltruistic approach *can* strengthen a state in certain ways and keep the trains running on time.

So as a practical matter, a leader needs to know where his ethical convictions begin to diverge from pure, cold self-interest. To help in that regard, let's consider a question which I have posed at times to newly minted graduates at commencement ceremonies at which I've been invited to speak. It is an extremely difficult and often quite personal and embarrassing question. No, it has nothing to do with sex. Rather, the question is: How do you feel about God?

I can almost imagine some members of the audience thinking to themselves, "Say what? Did he say God? Why would anyone bring up God at a commencement ceremony? Surely most of us, as modern intellectuals, have grown beyond the point at which God or our relationship to him is a serious question. And besides, I am a Jew, or a Baptist, or a Hindu, or a Catholic, and if you want to know how I feel about God you need only consult this prayer book or that scripture or this catechistic text."

I quickly assure the graduates that I'm not trying to sell them a set of religious beliefs. After all, the question is not how *should* you feel about God, but how *do* you feel about God in fact? A perfectly acceptable answer is that, deep down in your heart, you believe there is no God at all, or that there is a God but you simply don't wish to have a relationship with him.

What I have found, however, is that the vast majority of people—leaders and followers alike—duck this question altogether (in the same way that they avoid addressing the bus driver scenarios described at the beginning of this chapter). Discovering how one feels about God is simply too difficult or frightening for most people to address in any serious or meaningful way.

There are millions of people who regularly attend religious services, and yet haven't the foggiest idea of how they feel about God, or what kind of relationship they have with their God, or what they expect of him, or what they believe he expects of them. And similarly, there are millions of agnostics who have concluded that questions pertaining to God are simply unanswerable or unimportant, and yet find it impossible to fully suppress their concerns for the spiritual and transcendental aspects of their own existence.

As noted earlier, we are as fully human, and no more human, than our brothers and sisters in ancient Egypt or in modern Mongolia. And one of mankind's deepest and most abiding concerns for all times, in all places, and for all peoples, is our feeling for and relationship with God.

A leader may be able to run from his true feelings about God or non-God, but it is very difficult to hide from them in the long term. Thus it is probably to his advantage to discover and confront those feelings sooner rather than later. Doing so will almost certainly help him locate his moral center, and in the process help him become a better leader.

Are a leader's own moral preferences—say, a preference for being fully candid and honest—always the proper basis for guiding his followers in any and all situations? I would argue that they are not. But before you dismiss that view as moral relativism, I would also argue that the contrarian leader still must choose his moral course of action, moment by moment, and accept undiminished responsibility for the full scope and effect of his choices.

"Nothing is good or bad," Shakespeare wrote in *Hamlet*, "only thinking makes it so." Indeed, in a pluralistic society in which people have widely differing opinions about right and wrong, it takes courageous and discerning thought on the part of a leader to decide what is the most moral course of action for a particular situation.

A great many people, from political leaders to CEOs, subscribe to an amoral approach to leadership which focuses on technique and which avoids moral considerations altogether. For such people the bottom line is all that counts, or as Vince Lombardi said so pungently, "Winning's not the most important thing; it's the *only* thing!"

By contrast, only a handful of observers talk much about the ethical dimensions of leadership. Notable among this small group is James O'Toole, whose views are a useful launching pad for a discussion of "good" (i.e., morally sound) leadership.

O'Toole's excellent book *Leading Change* helps make the case for values-based leadership. As he notes in the preface to a recent edition, "Learning to lead is . . . not simply a matter of style, of how-to, of following some recipe, or even of mastering 'the vision thing.' Instead, leadership is about ideas and values," Here I heartily agree.

O'Toole goes on to argue, however, that a moral and ethical approach to leadership cannot coexist with "contingency leadership"—an approach which says that the best course of action is partly or entirely contingent on the circumstances. O'Toole contends that such an "it depends" philosophy amounts to moral relativism in the worst sense of the term. Here I must disagree.

There is of course nothing wrong with a leader holding on to his own deep-seated moral beliefs and consistently acting on the basis of those beliefs. But he must come to terms with the fact that the people with whom he must work effectively, including in some cases even his chief lieutenants, may have moral beliefs which differ sharply from his own. Is it the leader's job to try to impose his moral beliefs on his lieutenants and followers, or should he instead tolerate a diversity of moral views within his organization? And if the latter, how great a diversity?

O'Toole makes a strong case for there being an irreducible moral code which every good leader must adhere to. For example, O'Toole says that torture is always wrong and is never to be tolerated by a good leader, even if it could gain the leader information that would save the lives, or relieve the suffering, of thousands of his followers.

I am personally attracted to O'Toole's approach. But in the final analysis, I'm probably more tolerant than he is toward the differing moral values of my colleagues. After all, as the saying goes, "A man is never so provincial as when he begins to legislate for the universe."

For example, I feel that polygyny is morally wrong, but I recognize that a sizable fraction of the world's current population (and most of the social orders that have existed historically) would disagree with me. While my own views are strongly held, I would be disinclined to try to impose my aversion to polygyny on peoples for whom it is a time-honored and respected practice.

Admittedly, the demarcation between moral tolerance and moral relativism is not a bright line. My advice to contrarian leaders involves a delicate balancing act: Develop and hold your own moral convictions, while being as open as possible to the strongly held moral beliefs of others.

From time to time it is necessary for a leader to forthrightly condemn a colleague's or a follower's beliefs as being morally repugnant and just plain wrong. But almost as frequently, the contrarian leader will find that his own beliefs are being reshaped in part by the differing moral views of those around him. I see nothing intrinsically deleterious in this process, provided the leader always retains his intellectual and moral independence and takes personal responsibility for his actions.

Suppose an American politician were to say on the hustings:

> I am not, nor ever have been, in favor of bringing about, in any way, the social and political equality of the white and black races. . . . I am not, nor ever have been, in favor of making voters or jurors of Negroes, nor of qualifying them to hold office, nor of intermarrying with white people; and I will say, in addition to this, that there is a physical difference between the white and black races which I believe will forever forbid the two races living together on terms of political and social equality. And inasmuch as they cannot so live, while they do remain together, there must be the position of superior and inferior; and I, as much as any other man, am in favor of having the superior position assigned to the white race.

Outrageous? Yes! Racist? Absolutely! Morally repugnant? Without a doubt! But what happens when we learn that these very words were spoken by the Great Emancipator himself, Abraham Lincoln? Do we condemn Lincoln out of hand as a racist pig? Or do we continue to judge him as one of our greatest and most humane presidents by using a set of standards for our judgment that are more in keeping with the moral climate of his time?

I come down squarely for the latter approach, in which we judge Lincoln in the context of mid-nineteenth-century America. When we do so, he clearly emerges as one of the most morally uplifting leaders in history.

How tiresome it has become to hear various modern-day hypocrites attack the likes of Washington, Jefferson and Lincoln because they did things or believed things which most Americans today find unacceptable. Yes, Washington and Jefferson owned slaves, and yes, it would have been inconceivable to all three men that women should be allowed to vote or hold political office. But should those facts diminish their moral stature in the broad sweep of world history? Of course not.

One of my favorite historical leaders is George Washington. For all his warts and shortcomings, he more than any other person advanced the cause of liberal democracy in the modern world. He was indeed the American Cincinnatus—the man who refused the crown in order to give constitutional government, shorn of the trappings of monarchy, a chance to take root and flourish.

To reduce Washington or any other historical leader to pygmy status simply because he fails to meet the test of contemporary moral values is, in my judgment, sheer lunacy. In so doing we lose almost all of the models of excellence to which those of us who aspire to become good leaders can turn for guidance.

Ethical leadership requires that the leader choose one set of moral values over all others, and then take full responsibility for his actions based on those values. Such leaders are readily distinguishable from those who lead purely by expediency, who are, in the Tolstoyan sense, simply riding the crests of the waves of history, and whose long-term impact is usually minimal.

But the contrarian knows that the fact that a person is an ethical leader doesn't necessarily mean he's a good leader. Rather, distinguishing good leaders from bad ones requires that the person making the judgment choose a set of moral standards on which his judgment will be based. Here men and women of good will might differ sharply.

For example, to me Henry VIII was a morally depraved pig who murdered his wives, executed Thomas More, and indulged his voracious appetites with abandon, but most of the English I've met think of Henry as one of England's greatest kings. Similarly, I've always regarded Mao Tse-Tung as the all-time champion mass murderer, with estimates of his achievements in this regard approaching thirty million people killed, but many Chinese now regard Mao as one of the greatest leaders in Chinese history.

As much as most of us would like to deny it, moral and ethical concerns insinuate themselves into almost every aspect of leadership. And as has been pointed out so many times before, every leader must come to terms with his own moral beliefs and be held accountable in the end for the decisions he makes based on those beliefs. I'm reminded here of the words of a wise philosopher, my daughter Elizabeth, to the effect that moral leadership is less about what you're willing to live with than it is about what you're willing to die with.

Chapter 8

Work for Those
Who Work for You

One of my earliest introductions to real leadership occurred in 1971 when I was named (at the tender age of thirty) to be deputy director for academic affairs of the Illinois Board of Higher Education. There I learned a great deal from the board's chairman, George Clements, who had made a name for himself as the man who built the Chicago-based Jewel Tea Company into a major national grocery chain.

When I first arrived at my post, Mr. Clements said, "Steve, let me give you some basic advice about leadership. You should spend a small amount of your time hiring your direct reports, evaluating them, exhorting them, setting their compensation, praising them, kicking their butts and, when necessary, firing them. When you add all that up, it should come out to about 10 percent of your time. For the remaining 90 percent of your time you should be doing *everything you can* to help your direct reports succeed. You should be the first assistant to the people who work for you."

Powerful contrarian advice—and rarely followed. Even a leader who subscribes to contemporary democratic theories of management finds it difficult to think of his lieutenants as his equals, much less as his bosses. But that's exactly what Mr. Clements was saying: "Work for those who work for you!" If you're not in the process of getting rid of a lieutenant, bend over backward to help him get his job done. That means returning his phone calls promptly, listening carefully to his plans and problems, calling on others at his request, and helping him formulate his goals and develop strategies for achieving those goals. It's not simply that you should be your lieutenant's staff person, you should be his *best* staff person.

Virtually all leadership experts, whether they subscribe to traditional or *au courant* theories, depict leadership as a glamorous and majestic calling. But the contrarian isn't fooled. He knows that effective day-to-day leadership isn't so much about himself, as it is about the men and women he chooses to be his chief lieutenants. He knows that a lot of the things on his own plate will be minutiae and silliness, while his lieutenants will get to do the fun and important things.

If a would-be leader wants glamour, he should try acting in the movies. However, if he in fact wants to make a consequential impact on a cause or an organization, he needs to roll up his sleeves and be prepared to perform a series of grungy chores which are putatively beneath him, and for which he'll never receive recognition or credit, but by virtue of which his lieutenants will be inspired and enabled to achieve great things.

Teddy Roosevelt once observed, "The best executive is the one who recruits the most competent men around, tells them what he wants done, and then gets out of their way so they can do it." I buy that (if we include women as well as men), with the qualification that a leader should not merely get out of the way of his lieutenants, but actively assist them and forge them into an effective team.

Genghis Khan is widely recognized as one of the greatest politicians and military geniuses in history, having welded various nomadic tribes together into a unified Mongolian state, and then expanded his empire through conquest. But his most notable strength was his skill in finding excellent generals; that may in fact have been more important than anything else he did as a leader. Indeed, throughout history the greatest leaders have been not the ones who operated high above their subordinates, but rather the ones who could identify and recruit the best talent and marshal it effectively under a guiding and unifying vision.

Since so much of effective leadership involves bringing in the best talent possible, we should take note of an almost universal human truth: most people tend to hire people who are weaker than themselves. Moreover, this rule of thumb is nonlinear in practice—that is, excellent people tend to hire people only slightly weaker than themselves, while weak people tend to hire people who are much weaker than themselves. Or to paraphrase an old saw, "A's hire A-minuses, and B's hire C's."

Here it may be helpful to do a simple calculation based on a formula given to me by a former colleague, Harry Williams. Harry contended that people who are at the 99th percentile of overall competence will hire people who are only 99 percent as good as themselves—i.e., those who are, on an absolute scale, at the 98th percentile. These in turn will hire people who are only 98 percent as good as themselves—i.e., those who are only at the 96th percentile on an absolute scale of competence. Thus, according to Harry's Rule, if you start with someone at the top of an organization who is at the 99th percentile, the people at the fourth level in that organization will still be above the 92nd percentile of competence on an absolute scale.

But suppose the top person is only at the 90th percentile of competence. In accordance with Harry's Rule, he will hire people who are only 90 percent as good as he is—i.e., people who are at the 81st percentile on an absolute scale. They will in turn hire people at the 66th percentile, and thus the people at the fourth level of the organization will only be at the 43rd percentile of overall competence.

Harry's Rule is a good example of pseudoscience rising to the level of myth, which then helps us make sense of a complex human phenomenon. Strictly speaking, of course, overall competence is never unidimensional and can rarely be quantified. But Harry's Rule allows us to understand why it is so important to recruit the very best leaders to top-level positions in any organization, and why as a general rule the competence of the staff declines so rapidly as we descend the ranks of an organization whose top leader is only mediocre.

In an ideal world one would expect strong leaders to hire people who are superior to themselves. And in point of fact, many leaders do hire people who are more competent than themselves in specific areas of expertise. But in spite of all the lip service to the contrary, very few leaders are willing to appoint lieutenants whose overall competence exceeds their own. Ironically, in those rare instances in which a leader is in fact willing to hire people who are truly better than he is, the leader himself is generally not regarded at the time as a superstar (Mayor Richard Daley the elder and President Harry Truman come immediately to mind).

Thus one can rest assured that, in most organizations, Harry's Rule is in full swing. So it almost always makes sense to do whatever is necessary to attract and retain an outstanding *leader* (as opposed to a mere celebrity) for the very top position.

A somewhat contradictory approach to Harry's Rule in the appointment of lieutenants is what I like to call Dr. Hovde's Rule. In the spring of 1971, Fred Hovde was finishing the twenty-fifth and final year of his presidency of Purdue University. As a newly tenured associate professor of electrical engineering at Purdue, I had been awarded a national fellowship to serve a one-year term as an administrative intern with Dr. Hovde.

As we walked across the campus one day, President Hovde explained to me how he was agonizing over whether to appoint a particular person to fill a key vacancy in his administration. I naïvely asked him if he thought this candidate were "the right man for the job." And Hovde stopped and said, "Steve, that's the wrong question to ask. There's no such thing as 'the right man for the job.' The appropriate question to ask is, 'Is he the best man available for the job within the time frame in which I must fill the position?'"

Hovde went on to note that a near superstar is the wrong person for a particular job if someone better is available. And conversely, a truly mediocre candidate may be the right person for the job if he's better than anyone else who's available, and if you absolutely must fill the position right away.

Now we can begin to understand one of the trickiest parts of major-league leadership—the inevitable trade-off between whom we'd *like* to have as a lieutenant, and who can actually be recruited within the time that's available for making the appointment. In that sense, choosing lieutenants is simply another instance in which the leader must make decisions under conflicting constraints (as discussed in Chapter 5).

In particular, if the pickings are slim, the leader must ask herself if she can delay filling the position beyond the time originally allotted, in the hope that someone better might become available. Or she may decide to redesign the vacancy to take advantage of an existing candidate's special strengths, while pawning off to others of her lieutenants some of the responsibilities originally assigned to the vacant position.

One of the silliest things a leader can do is to first rigidly define the responsibilities of a position, and then try to find a human being to match this preconceived job description. It's as though the leader believed that talented people were being stamped out by a machine to fulfill certain mechanical specifications. To the extent permitted by law and opportunity, a leader is often better served by recruiting a really competent lieutenant, and then tailoring a set of responsibilities to fit the strengths of that particular person. Contrarian leaders know that it's great people, not great job descriptions, that make an organization successful.

A primary challenge for any leader is to surround himself with people whose skills make up for his own shortcomings. This is much easier said than done, because most leaders are more comfortable being surrounded by people who are similar to the leader himself. In particular, it is seductively easy for an entrenched leader to choose and retain only lieutenants who always agree with him and never seriously resist his initiatives. But the long-term success of any organization demands that the leader not surround himself with yes-men and sycophants.

A related factor in the choosing of lieutenants is age. I recently turned sixty, so I'd be the last person in the world to favor or practice age discrimination. But time and again I have been advised by successful leaders that, between two roughly equal candidates, one should always choose the younger.

As the leader of an organization ages, his lieutenants and the entire organization tend to age with him. The leader begins filling open positions with people whose life experiences (and length of life) are roughly equal to his own. Before he knows it, a reverse age discrimination can occur in which it becomes difficult to bring younger people into the inner circle. The fresh perspective that almost invariably accompanies youth soon vanishes, unless the leader makes a conscious effort to recruit and promote young turks.

I was appointed executive vice president of the University of Nebraska at age thirty-three. As I neared forty, my mentors and colleagues began to urge me to throw my hat in the ring for various university presidencies. As I pursued several of these opportunities I began to sense that my age was working against me. I might make it to the final three or four candidates, but then I could just feel the trustees (most of whom were over sixty) saying among themselves, "He's only thirty-nine; he's still a kid; he's not *old enough* to be a university president!"

However, when I actually turned forty, it was as though I had suddenly become a full-grown man, sufficiently mature to carry a spear and assume the mantle of presidential leadership. I was in fact the same person I had been a few months before, but in the eyes of those making the decision I was a completely different person. Within a year I was appointed president of the flagship campus of the SUNY System after turning down a couple of other presidential offers.

Ironically, nearly fifteen years later I was discussing with some of my senior colleagues the pros and cons of a particular decanal candidate who was not yet forty. I was about to say the man was far too young to be a dean, when I recalled with embarrassment that he was just about the age I was when I first became a university president.

When setting out to fill an open position for a lieutenant, one should not give the job to an outside candidate simply because he or she appears to be slightly better than the leading inside candidate. Derek Bok, the distinguished former president of Harvard, pointed out to me that because you already know an inside candidate's shortcomings and blemishes, an outside candidate must be at least two notches above the leading insider in order to be a good risk.

After all, no matter how many reference checks you make, the outsider exists largely on paper, while the insider is a flesh-and-blood person whom you've seen perform in the heat of battle. You already know the situations in which you have faith in the insider's abilities and the situations in which you don't. We're often attracted to the outsider because he seems nearly perfect, while in fact he has as many flaws as any other human being but we simply have not yet discovered what they are.

The foregoing advice must be tempered by the advantages attendant to bringing fresh blood into an organization. If a leader's cadre of senior lieutenants has become moribund, and if they in turn have anesthetized several layers of their own subordinates, then it behooves the leader to appoint outsiders, even though the outsiders may not appear to be quite as good as the leading insiders. In such cases the need for a transfusion of fresh blood takes precedence over the candidates' nominal credentials.

Achieving real diversity among one's senior lieutenants is a *very* difficult task. Differences that have been culturally important for a long period of time are hardly ever simply "skin deep." Integrating one's organization—whether it be with respect to race, gender, ethnicity or political persuasion—requires a great deal of hard work and patience, and a willingness to try and try again after repeated setbacks.

Yet the advantages of real diversity are usually worth the pain and costs involved. A highly homogeneous organization is as susceptible to disease and infestations as is a large biological monoculture. Every farmer knows that when he and his neighbors plant tens of thousands of contiguous acres in a particular variety of wheat year after year, that variety will soon become vulnerable to new diseases or new strains of insects. Ecosystems that are biologically diverse are much tougher and more resilient in the long run than monocultures, and so it is with organizations that contain a wide variety of people working toward a common goal.

Moreover, a leader's self-interests are often well served by recruiting people who conventional wisdom would say should be excluded from consideration. When I was a boy it was a settled fact that no black man could ever be the quarterback of a champion football team ("they're not smart enough"), and no woman could ever run a university or a corporation ("they're not tough enough"). Most of us would laugh at such stereotypes today, but fifty years ago they created nearly insurmountable barriers to extraordinarily competent and highly motivated minorities and women. These people often delivered outstanding performances for the few contrarian leaders who were willing to give them a fair chance. Walter O'Malley, the owner of the Brooklyn Dodgers baseball team, took a lot of heat when he brought Jackie Robinson into the majors in 1947, but in the end O'Malley was richly rewarded for his troubles.

The contrarian leader understands the difference between statistics and stereotypes. He knows there can be significant statistical differences in the performance of two groups of people on a particular test, and at the same time significant overlap between the two groups. The key factor for the leader to keep in mind is that he's hiring an individual human being, not a group or a stereotype.

Most Americans alive today believe that race and gender are the major barriers that separate us, in large part because our politicians and the popular media are constantly playing up (and playing off) these differences. And to be sure, it's not easy to weld men and women of different races and ethnicities into a cohesive team.

But the contrarian leader knows it's even harder to weld together a group of lieutenants who *think* differently from one another. In the long run the most difficult part of building a diverse team of lieutenants is to integrate people whose intellectual and moral perspectives cover a wide spectrum and are not simply isomorphic with those of the leader.

One of the greatest gifts a leader can give his line officers—i.e., those with direct responsibility for actually running the organization—is protection from the leader's support staff. Untold amounts of needless mischief and ill will are caused every day by well-intentioned secretaries and "assistants to." Indeed, it's not uncommon for a leader ultimately to be undone by such folk.

Don't get me wrong. During my time as a leader I have been blessed with truly remarkable and dedicated support staff, without whom my office would quickly have ground to a halt. Nonetheless, staff members—in any kind of organization—can cause more problems than would at first glance seem possible.

Whenever a staff person is empowered to act as a buffer between a leader and his line officers, the results can be truly disastrous. The primary reason is that, under these circumstances, the staff person can exercise the power of the leader while being shielded from the heat and accountability that should always attend the exercise of power. This particular kind of occult authority can be especially seductive; even the most honest and selfless staff person can become addicted to it. Before he's even aware of it himself, the staffer begins to manipulate the line officers, block their access to the leader, and subtly distort communications twixt leader and line.

Back in 1970, Robert Townsend, the man who built Avis Rent-a-Car into a highly profitable competitor to Hertz ("When you're Number Two, you try harder"), wrote a book entitled *Up the Organization*. This book has had a powerful effect on my development as a contrarian leader. Townsend compellingly described the dangers of support staff in any organization. He was extremely proud of the fact that he was able to run a large and complex corporation with neither a secretary nor an assistant.

I'm not as brave as Townsend (i.e., I still use support staff), but I've tried to marry his philosophy with that of George Clements (cited at the beginning of this chapter): to wit, that the leader *and his staff* are there to support the line officers, not the other way around.

I first became aware of the problems associated with support staff early on in my career, when I realized how much they could control access to my boss. In the process, they often interfered with my ability to do my job. Moreover, my having to kowtow to my boss's staff both angered and humiliated me.

By contrast, I make certain that the line officers who are my direct reports have unfettered access to me—twenty-four hours a day, seven days a week, no questions asked. If a senior vice president calls my office, the assistant answering the call will tell him where I am and what I'm doing, and will then immediately say, "If you need to talk with Steve right now, I'll be glad to get him for you."

It doesn't matter whether I'm in Tokyo or sick at home or courting a donor or meeting with a group of trustees, the assistant always says the same thing: "If you need to talk with Steve right now, I'll get him for you." She never asks, "What do you want to talk with him about?" nor does she say, "I'm sorry, he's busy and can't speak with you right now." In other words, the decision as to whether or not my assistant should interrupt me is vested in the line officer, not in the assistant.

When I share this concept with other leaders, they always shudder and say, "Gosh, Steve, you must be inundated with interruptions." But in nearly twenty years as a university president, I think I've been peremptorily interrupted by my direct reports no more than twenty times. How can that be? Why would officers who enjoy unrestricted license to interrupt their boss at any time use that privilege so sparingly in practice?

The answer has three parts. First, the senior officers and I meet together once a week, and I meet with each officer individually once every week or two. Most matters can wait to be discussed at one of these regular meetings.

Second, when my assistant tells a senior officer, "Steve's meeting with so-and-so," or "he's asleep in Tokyo," or whatever, the officer almost invariably says, "Oh, don't disturb him. Perhaps he could call me when he's free." The outcome in such cases is the same as if the staffer had said, "I'm sorry, Steve's busy right now, so he'll have to call you back." The difference (and it's a big difference) is that the officer, not the staffer, decided that the matter could wait.

Third, unlike a lot of leaders, I'm not afraid of my direct reports. I don't need an assistant to carry out the harsher aspects of my job for me. If in my judgment an officer who has interrupted me is wasting my time, I'll tell him so in no uncertain terms. And he knows that if he does it too often, I'll get rid of him. But as long as he's one of my chief lieutenants, I'll never restrict his access to me.

I grew up watching *I Remember Mama*, a 1950s television series based on a book by Kathryn Forbes entitled *Mama's Bank Account*. Peggy Woods played the matriarch of a Norwegian family living in San Francisco in the early twentieth century. The family's resources were meager at best and often inadequate, but Mama always reassured the children by telling them she had $500 (a large sum in those days) in a bank account downtown in case they ever ran into real trouble. When they fell into difficult straits, the family would discuss raiding Mama's bank account, but in the end they always decided they could scrape by and leave the nest egg alone. After the children were all grown, Mama informed them that there was not and never had been any $500 bank account; there was no nest egg. Yet the mere idea that there was one had been enough to get them through.

In a sense, when senior officers know they can always and instantly reach the president, it gives them a *real* Mama's bank account. They're glad they have it, but they almost always decide they don't need to use it. Yet the very fact that they have unfettered access to the president can give them tremendous leverage in working with others in the university or with prospective donors or governmental agencies.

A corollary of the foregoing approach is that a leader should never convey direct orders to senior officers through staff. It's too easy for the intervening staffer to slightly modify the order, either inadvertently or intentionally. Besides, conveying orders *through* staff can make the senior officers feels as though they're taking orders *from* staff.

Of course I do ask my staff to collect information from, or pass along information to, the senior officers, and these officers in turn often use my staff for the same purposes. But when an important directive needs to be given to a senior lieutenant, it comes straight from me—either in person or by phone, memo, handwritten note, fax, or e-mail.

Occasionally an historian will argue that a particular king was intrinsically a great leader, but that his reign was tarnished by incompetent ministers. In this same vein I've often overheard people in organizations say apologetically that their leader is outstanding, but he's hampered by terrible secretaries, ministers, lieutenants or assistants. Nonsense! A good leader has no excuse for having incompetent lieutenants and staff. As Machiavelli observed, a principe with weak advisers is a weak principe.

A few weeks after being named executive vice president of the University of Nebraska in 1974, I placed a call to the chairman of a particular department on one of our campuses. Following Robert Townsend's advice, I placed the call myself (a practice I have followed religiously for thirty years). Without using my title, I said, "This is Steven Sample calling. May I please speak with Dr. Smith?" His secretary replied, "I'm sorry, Dr. Smith is very busy at the moment and cannot take your call." I said, "Fine. Would you please have him call Steven Sample when he's free?" "No," she said, "I can't do that." Puzzled, I asked why not. She said, "Dr. Smith doesn't return calls. You'll just have to call again." By this time it was obvious to me that she thought I was "merely" a student. I asked, "But what if he's still busy?" "Well then," she said matter-of-factly, "you'll just have to call again and again until you reach him." Exasperated, I said, "Look, I'm not going to do that. Just tell Dr. Smith that Steven Sample called and that I . . ." She cut me off and said, "No, I can't even give him your message. I'm sorry, those are the rules." And with that she hung up.

After cooling down a bit I did a little office work, went home to a nice dinner with my wife, and then waited until 1:00 in the morning to call the man at his home. To the startled and groggy department chair, I said, "Dr. Smith, this is Executive Vice President Steven Sample calling. I couldn't get through your secretary today, even though I really needed to talk to you. But since you're so damned busy and important, I thought you might be available to talk with me at 1:00 A.M." I then added, "Look, Smith, why would you have a policy of not returning phone calls and not receiving messages? Why would you let your staff treat anybody like that?"

Not surprisingly, Smith decided to resign his department chairmanship shortly thereafter. But the point of the story is that I didn't blame his secretary's incredible rudeness and insensitivity on the secretary; rather, I blamed it all on Smith. After all, the secretary was simply carrying out Smith's policies.

Like anyone who writes about leadership, I'm tempted to claim that if a leader follows an approach to leadership which I find to be morally acceptable, he will succeed; and if he eschews such an approach, he is doomed to ignominious failure. But I'll be honest:

there are many approaches to leadership that succeed even though I personally disapprove of them.

For example, while it's extremely important to me that my direct reports trust me, I must confess that there have been many effective leaders who were not trusted by their senior lieutenants. It's probably important that the rank-and-file of the leader's followers trust him, but the same need not be true of his chief lieutenants.

Franklin Roosevelt and Joseph Stalin are two important illustrations of this point. FDR loved the American public and enjoyed their trust in return, but he misled his chief lieutenants on a daily basis. These advisers would leave a meeting convinced that FDR had a specific belief or intent, only to find he had something else entirely in mind. Working with him was not easy.

Similarly, while the Soviet citizenry for the most part trusted Stalin, his own subordinates most certainly did not. Indeed, Stalin may have been one of the most untrustworthy leaders in history, but one could hardly say he was ineffective.

I myself have worked very effectively under leaders whom I didn't trust, didn't like, and didn't respect. It's not fun, but it can under certain circumstances work amazingly well. I remember a colleague once telling me that it was a mark of maturity to be able to work effectively under an untrustworthy leader.

Nonetheless, as a general rule I think it's much to be preferred for a leader to earn and receive the trust of his principal lieutenants, and for them to earn and receive the leader's trust in return. Life is too short to do otherwise.

We've talked at length about how to hire lieutenants and how to support them in their work. But now we come to one of the most painful aspects of leadership: firing lieutenants. One of the best insights I ever gained in this area came from the farm, not from the classroom or the boardroom.

When I was six years old my family moved from St. Louis to a farm outside the city—complete with farmhouse and outbuildings, forty acres of land, a few cattle, hogs, and chickens, two riding horses, and a goat. Because my father was born and bred a city boy, and because he still worked in town, he relied frequently on the advice and assistance of our farmer neighbor, Percy Gillette.

One day my family returned home from a shopping trip to find that the goat had gotten into our house and wreaked havoc. My mother insisted then and there that the goat had to go. Dad called up Percy and asked him how one went about getting rid of a goat. Percy said, "It's easy, Howard. Just bring it over here and I'll show you." Dad brought the goat over, Percy hit it over the head with a sledgehammer, and the job was done.

A few months later it was time for one of our hogs to be butchered, and Dad again turned to Percy for help. He said, "No problem, Howard, just bring it over and I'll take care of it." So we brought the hog over to Percy and he personally slit its throat and butchered it.

Some time later my brother and I were out riding our horses when my brother's horse badly injured itself by stepping into a gopher hole. A veterinarian came out to our farm the next day, and after examining the horse he told us that its leg was broken and that it would have to be destroyed.

Dad again went to Percy and asked for his assistance. But this time Percy was horrified. "Howard," he said, "I couldn't shoot one of your horses. A horse is different. It's not a hog or a steer or a goat. I'd sooner dishonor another man's wife than shoot his horse. Besides, if you got someone else to shoot that horse for you, you'd never be able to hold your head up around these parts. A man has to shoot his own horse, Howard. He owes it to the horse."

As far as I know, my father, the city boy, had never shot any living thing in his life. But early the next morning Dad went outside with a shotgun as the rest of us huddled in the living room. We heard two loud reports, and then my father walked back into the house, white as a sheet. He quickly drank three fingers of whiskey and went back to bed.

It was a powerful contrarian lesson: *A man has to shoot his own horse, because he owes it to the horse.* Doesn't a leader similarly owe it to his lieutenants to fire them himself?

The world is full of squeamish leaders when it comes to getting rid of people. Like the airline president described in Chapter 2 who lacks the guts to respond personally to letters of complaint, many leaders simply can't bring themselves to look a chief lieutenant in the eye and tell him he has to go. President Richard Nixon was notorious in this regard. After winning reelection by a huge margin in 1972, he reportedly sent his hatchet man, Bob Haldeman, to tell the senior staff that the president had decided he needed a new team.

Actually, the contrarian leader knows that firing your lieutenants yourself can often pay big dividends. Some years back there was a bank CEO in California who was famous for being loved and respected by the people he had let go. In one instance he fired one of his best friends by calling the man into his office, looking him straight in the eye and saying, "Bill, you and I are good friends. We've been fishin' together and we've been whorin' together, but there's no place for you anymore in this bank." This CEO was brutally honest when he had to convey bad news to a lieutenant, but he was never insincere or condescending. Moreover, he never humiliated a person by sending bad news through an intermediary. Thus the lieutenants still on board at the bank always knew their jobs were secure unless and until the CEO himself told them otherwise.

A close cousin to firing lieutenants yourself is evaluating them yourself. Every senior lieutenant deserves a complete and frank evaluation by the leader at least once a year. It should be clear to the lieutenant that the leader has spent a good deal of time thinking through the evaluation, and that the leader has taken pains to identify the lieutenant's achievements and failures as measured against the goals that the lieutenant and the leader had agreed to at the preceding evaluation.

The foregoing advice is so elementary as to be almost insulting to any practicing leader or student of leadership. What's so contrarian about evaluating your subordinates on a regular basis? Every leader does that, right?

Wrong! Oh, it's certainly true that almost every leader goes through some kind of elaborate process for evaluating her direct reports each year, often conducted at great expense under the supervision of a high-priced consultant. But what the average leader doesn't do is sit down and devote several hours of her own time each year to really thinking through a particular lieutenant's achievements and shortcomings, and then communicating those thoughts face to face to the lieutenant. Moreover, the average leader doesn't ask each lieutenant to prepare an in-depth self-assessment of his (the lieutenant's) own performance, and then listen carefully to the lieutenant as he describes his self-assessment and contrasts it with the leader's assessment of the lieutenant.

An extra benefit of candid assessments by a leader of her lieutenants is that the leader can often get an officer to leave on his own accord without firing him. I've sometimes said to a direct report of mine, "Russ, I really would like you out of here. In my judgment both you and the university would benefit by a change. But please understand, I'm not firing you; rather, I'm leaving the decision completely up to you." In almost every case the person has left shortly thereafter, but in a manner that makes it credible that he left of his own accord.

Elaborate consultant-driven assessment schemes are fine. But the contrarian leader knows they are no substitute for hard thinking about a particular lieutenant's performance and potential by both the leader and the lieutenant, followed by an extensive face-to-face no-holds-barred conversation between the two. It's really every bit as important, and no more difficult, than shooting your own horse.

Some leaders believe they can foster a healthy competitive spirit within their organization by pitting their chief lieutenants against one another. Other leaders encourage rivalries among lieutenants on the theory that subordinates who are constantly fighting each other are in no position to stage a coup against the leader. FDR certainly permitted his cabinet officers to wage war among themselves; Lincoln also had warring cabinet members, not because he encouraged it, but because he was unable to control it.

The "let 'em fight it out" approach to team building among one's senior lieutenants may yield short-term benefits in certain circumstances. But as mentioned in Chapter 5, a better approach in the long term is for the leader to resolve disputes among his senior officers before such disputes lead to permanent animosities.

I certainly encourage my senior vice presidents to try to work through their differences on their own. But I make it clear that they have an obligation to bring the matter to me for resolution whenever one of the disputants feels that an impasse has been reached. Moreover, it is a cardinal sin in our culture for one disputant to retaliate against another simply because the latter felt it was time to refer the matter in dispute to me.

The foregoing approach allows a healthy amount of give-and-take among the senior officers with a minimum of protracted trench warfare. As with Mama's bank account, simply knowing that I'm ready and willing to resolve disputes upon application by any one officer puts pressure on all officers to expeditiously work things out among themselves.

As a practical matter, I doubt that more than five or six issues a year are referred to me for resolution through this process. This low number may be due in part to the fact that my senior officers know I would cheerfully fire one or more of them if they were consistently unable to resolve their differences among themselves.

Under what circumstances should a leader sacrifice himself to protect his chief lieutenants? Under what circumstances should he sacrifice his chief lieutenants to protect himself?

These are painfully complicated questions. Personally, I believe that a leader should be willing to sacrifice himself or one or more principal lieutenants for the sake of the cause or organization. However, things get sticky when a leader ostensibly sacrifices a lieutenant for the sake of the organization, but in fact is doing so simply to save the leader's own skin. Under these circumstances he quickly loses the confidence and respect of his lieutenants. Conversely, when a leader demonstrates a willingness to sacrifice not only his lieutenants but even himself for the sake of the organization or the cause, he gains moral credibility in the eyes of those he leads.

Let's consider a practical example. When Stanford University was attacked by the federal government in 1991 for alleged improprieties in the charging of overhead costs on federal research grants, Stanford's president at the time, Donald Kennedy, quickly and courageously stepped forward, took full responsibility for any wrongdoing, and became the principal lightning rod for the entire affair. This approach was certainly costly for Dr. Kennedy (he announced his resignation within the year). But more important, it may have been a mistake from the standpoint of protecting the university's interests.

In retrospect, it probably would have been better if Kennedy had pushed some other Stanford officer out on the point, and held himself in reserve. As it was, by committing the university's eight-hundred-pound gorilla at the outset of the battle, Stanford was left with no *masse de manœuvre* with which to counter the government's continuing assaults. Thus, in this case the brave and courageous approach of sacrificing the leader right off the bat may have worked against the university's best interests in the long term.

To a large degree, leaders live and die through the actions of their chief lieutenants. Choosing these people, motivating them, supporting them, helping them grow and achieve, inspiring them, evaluating them and firing them are among the most important things a leader does. When he carries out these duties well, his cause or organization has a good chance of flourishing. But if he fails at these essential (and unglamorous) tasks, he and his followers are almost certainly doomed to failure in the long run.

Thus Mr. Clements's advice at the beginning of this chapter—that a leader should be the first assistant to his chief lieutenants—isn't just sentimental pap; rather, it's sound advice in the self-interest of the leader.

Chapter 9

Follow the Leader

definition

Many thoughtful people consider Eleanor Roosevelt to have been an outstanding leader, but as a contrarian I must respectfully disagree. It's not that I have anything against Mrs. Roosevelt; on the contrary, I consider her to be an exemplary human being who exerted great influence during her lifetime. But I'm not at all certain it's helpful to categorize her as a *leader*.

As noted in the introduction to this book, when an author discusses leaders and leadership it's essential that he be clear as to his definitions. My definition of a leader is someone who has identifiable followers over whom he exercises power and authority through his actions and decisions. In Chapter 5, I noted that one of the tests of a leader's importance is whether anyone is really affected by, or cares about, the decisions he makes. Mrs. Roosevelt was noble, respected and influential, and she challenged prevailing views about equality and justice; but as far as I can tell she never had identifiable followers over whom she exercised power and authority.

Many great religious leaders have lacked formal or institutional power and authority, but such leaders have been able to exercise effective control of their followers by virtue of the leaders' putative relationship with God. Other people exercise power and authority over followers by virtue of elective or appointive office, or through great skill in combat, or by having a compelling

141

vision. But whatever the basis of his authority may be, when an effective leader turns in a new direction his followers turn with him; that's the test of real leadership. To paraphrase Harry Truman, leadership involves getting others to willingly move in a new direction in which they're not naturally inclined to move on their own.

In this chapter we'll examine the relationships between leaders and followers, and how it is that the former come to have power and authority over the latter. We'll also consider how it is that followers sometimes lead their leaders.

Before one can lead, one must acquire a set of followers; indeed, followers are the *sine qua non* of leadership. Sometimes a person is appointed to a position, such as CEO of a corporation, which comes complete with ready-made followers (e.g., the employees) who have little or no role in the selection of their leader. At other times a person (such as a civil rights leader) must build a set of followers from scratch. And quite often in democratic societies a would-be leader must convince a group of potential followers (e.g., the citizens of a country) to choose him as their chief. However, the contrarian leader understands that in all three cases the personality and reputation of the aspirant are often more important than his leadership skills in determining whether or not he gets the opportunity to lead.

For example, in the spring of 1984, at the height of the presidential primary election season, Democratic candidate Senator Gary Hart of Colorado burst out of obscurity to nearly topple the frontrunner and eventual party nominee, Walter Mondale. Although Hart ultimately was defeated, the youthful, intelligent and Kennedyesque senator had served notice that he would be a presence on the national stage in the coming years. Sure enough, in the spring of 1987, during the early stages of the 1988 presidential race, Hart enjoyed a commanding lead in the polls over all other candidates. But then the wheels suddenly fell off his campaign. Photos in the *National Enquirer* tabloid exposed an alleged

affair with a young model named Donna Rice, and within days
the embattled senator withdrew from the race. He bitterly pinned
the blame for his failed candidacy on the media, and after a short-
lived effort to restart his campaign a few months later, he again
accused the media of drawing attention away from his positions
on serious national issues in order to delve into the seamier details
of his personal life.

In retrospect, Hart's protest at the time of his downfall was
naïve and a bit foolish. The contrarian leader knows that an effective salesman must sell himself first and the product second, and
that similarly, an effective leader must sell himself first and his
vision or policies second. Hart allowed his candidacy to be torpe-
doed because he failed to recognize this simple reality.

One could make the case that Bill Clinton, unlike Gary Hart,
survived a similar scandal in the 1992 presidential campaign
because he shrewdly used the moment as an opportunity to sell
himself to the American voting public as a well-meaning man
who was committed to overcoming his personal shortcomings.
Then, once in power, Clinton was able to use the prestige and the
bully pulpit of the presidency to weather a whole series of scandals that dwarfed the preelection brouhaha which attended the
denouement of his affair with Gennifer Flowers.

Many would-be leaders intentionally seek out a leadership
post with a well-established podium or bully pulpit. The instant
credibility which inheres in such a podium or pulpit can add the
illusion of an additional twenty IQ points to the incumbent, and
even a measure of charm and good looks. I know that my words
carry more weight when I speak from the podium of the USC
presidency than they would if I were speaking simply as an electrical engineer from a small farm in Missouri, because my position
at the university carries with it a large number of loyal and powerful followers and supporters. Contrarian wisdom teaches that in
such cases it is the followers and supporters who give credence to
the leader, especially prior to his having demonstrated his ability
to lead.

General George C. Marshall, FDR's brilliant military chief of staff during World War II (and later a member of Truman's cabinet), once argued that "a leader in a democracy must also be an entertainer." Marshall himself didn't seem overly entertaining, but he made a compelling point nonetheless. Even inside well-defined hierarchies such as the military, the ability of a leader to entertain his constituents is important. As Warren Bennis has observed, effective leaders manage people's attention, and that requires some degree of entertainment skill.

Franklin Roosevelt exemplified this kind of leadership; as noted in Chapter 1, Orson Welles once assured the president that he was every bit as gifted a performing artist as Welles himself. Corporate icons such as Lee Iaccoca are often excellent entertainers, as are most professional politicians. And we can certainly include under this rubric Generals George Patton and Douglas MacArthur, both of whom enjoyed influence outside the military in part because of their ability to entertain the public through the use and manipulation of panache and symbols.

A colleague of mine who was named president of a large university some years ago came to me seeking advice on how to connect effectively with her constituents. We talked at some length about thinking gray, thinking free, artful listening, and choosing lieutenants. Then I told her, "Try starting your speeches with a good joke or anecdote." In other words, I urged her to become an accomplished entertainer.

A leader's ability to comfortably tell jokes and humorous anecdotes is important because it tends to make him appear warm and accessible (even when he's not). Among U.S. presidents, Lincoln, Kennedy and Reagan clearly had this ability, and Nixon and Carter clearly didn't.

But General Marshall's remark about the entertainment aspects of leadership goes much deeper than that. Indeed, the contrarian leader knows that telling compelling stories is one of the most powerful tools there is for establishing a close bond with his followers and for inculcating his vision among them.

The most effective leader in history in this regard was Jesus. The stories and parables which he used to teach his followers are as fresh and appealing today as they were two thousand years ago. One need not be a Christian to appreciate the tremendous power of the stories of the Good Samaritan or the Prodigal Son.

An important asset for any leader to have as he works to inspire and motivate his followers is a credible creation story or myth for the organization or movement he's leading. In my own case I took several years to propound and polish such a story for USC. In its most current version it runs as follows:

USC had its beginnings in a little white frame building that still stands at the entrance to our University Park campus. That was all there was to the University of Southern California when it was founded in 1880—one little building, fifty students, and twelve teachers. And keep in mind that at that time, Los Angeles was a dusty little village of ten thousand people.

But shortly thereafter, L.A. began to explode. It went from a village of ten thousand to a megacity of ten million in just over a century, which represents a thousand-fold increase in population. No other city in history has grown from ten thousand to ten million in one hundred years.

USC also exploded during that period in both size and complexity. A student body of fifty became a student body of twenty-eight thousand today. The net worth of USC in 1880 was $15,000; today our net worth exceeds $3 billion.

Now here is an interesting point. Several other colleges were established in this region in the 1880s, and some of these had better financial underpinnings than USC. But they didn't grow into national research universities like USC; rather, they remained small colleges.

What was it about USC that made us so different? Was it our name? Think of the chutzpah it took to put such a pretentious name—"The University of Southern California"—over the door of a little white frame building in 1880. Who was kidding whom? But if it wasn't just the name, then what was it? Dreams? Leadership? Serendipity?

Not only has USC grown dramatically over the last 120 years, but our role and mission have evolved as well. From 1880 to the 1950s, we were serving primarily a local clientele and playing a quasi-land-grant role. Of course we weren't a land-grant university, but we were serving public needs in the way that traditional land-grant universities do. Why? Because there wasn't anyone else in Southern California to do it, since public higher education in this state was largely locked up in Northern California.

But by the late 1950s all that had changed. USC's new president at the time, Norman Topping, saw that our quasi-land-grant role was being taken over, and properly so, by strong public universities. Topping understood that USC needed a new role, and that that new role would necessarily involve USC's becoming a national university, an endowed university and a research university.

This new role has been aggressively pursued for the past forty years during the presidencies of Topping, Jack Hubbard, Jim Zumberge and myself, with spectacular success. USC today is clearly a major national research university with a large permanent endowment.

The foregoing creation story has the virtue of being absolutely true, but many effective creation stories of companies, movements and nations are simply myths which are not easily falsifiable. Washington at Valley Forge, Adam and Eve in Eden, Newton watching the apple fall from the tree, Rosa Parks on the bus in Alabama, Romulus and Remus being nursed by the she-wolf, Bill Hewlett and Dave Packard in their garage—all are powerful and effective creation stories, and some of them are probably true. But the real test is that such stories must appeal strongly to the leader's followers and to those whom he is trying to recruit.

The USC creation story wasn't fashioned out of whole cloth by me; rather, I built on the creation stories used by my predecessor presidents. The story has a classic American heroic component (the "log cabin" leitmotif—up from humble beginnings), coupled with a few surprising facts and superlatives. It can be readily shortened or lengthened for different situations; for example, I sometimes add that USC was initially founded as a Methodist university by a group of three businessmen comprising a Jew, a Catholic and an Episcopalian; or that, in contrast to most other private universities, USC has freely and proudly admitted minorities and women to every one of its programs since its founding in 1880.

Most important of all, the USC creation story has been widely read, heard and internalized by a broad spectrum of the university's constituents. Like reassuring family stories told around the dinner table or fireplace, members of the Trojan Family (i.e., USC's students and their parents, faculty, staff, alumni, donors and friends) love to hear the university's creation story told again and again. I myself have probably told some version of the story to various audiences nearly a thousand times over the past decade, and no one appears to be tired of it.

Another important element of the USC creation story is that it embodies and ennobles the concept of change, thereby laying the groundwork for further changes in the future. Keep in mind that leadership is all about getting followers to move in new directions; thus, a creation story that enshrines the status quo is not much help to a leader.

Finally, the story engenders pride among the members of the Trojan Family; it inspires people to dream more audaciously than they might otherwise have done. After all, if a tiny little college with no resources to speak of, and located in a backwater village, can become an internationally renowned research university in just over a hundred years, what might the next hundred bring?

Effective leaders are able to create, manipulate and exemplify not only stories but symbols, slogans, and mantras as well. All of these help define in the minds of followers the essence of the leader's vision and his character.

Moreover, the leader often becomes a symbol in and of himself. His actions tell followers a great deal about who he is and where he's taking the organization. Or as Emerson put it, "Your actions speak so loudly I cannot hear what you say."

For me, teaching a course each year in electromagnetic theory or literature or leadership has been seen as a powerful symbol by many of my constituents, especially faculty, students and parents. Staying on campus and being visible night and day during the Los Angeles riots of 1992 (see Chapter 5) was also a powerful symbolic act that helped define my presidency. One can soon begin to appreciate how the queen of England must feel as the symbol of an entire nation.

At USC, a particularly important mantra involves the scope and power of the legendary Trojan Family, the university's lifelong and worldwide community of students, parents, alumni, faculty, staff and supporters. Our vice president for public relations, Martha Harris, helped me understand this point when she briefed me for the December 1990 press conference at which my appointment as USC's tenth president was first made public. "What should I say?" I asked her. "Trojan Family," she replied. "No, Martha, I mean what should I say to the media?" "Just stress the Trojan Family over and over," she urged me. "Try to make it impossible for the radio or TV people to create a sound bite of your remarks that doesn't include the words *Trojan Family*." I took her advice and was well-rewarded for having done so.

George Washington, while not an especially articulate man, was quite adept at creating and manipulating symbols. I recall reading an eyewitness account of Washington giving a talk shortly after the Revolutionary War to a group of disgruntled military officers who were angry that they had not been paid by the Continental Congress, and who were considering taking over the government by force. Washington was stumbling a bit while reading a relatively dry and uninspiring speech in which he urged the rebellious officers to cool down and reconsider their course of action. Suddenly he stopped, fumbled in his waistcoat for his spectacles, put them on and said, "You must excuse me, gentlemen. I've grown gray in the service of my country, and now I am going blind." Every man in the room got tears in his eyes, and the incipient rebellion melted away. It was the spectacles that did it.

Washington notwithstanding, the great majority of effective leaders have an excellent command of language, either spoken or written or both. Words are the primary stock-in-trade of leadership, and all leaders use them to attract, hold, inspire and galvanize their followers.

To be sure, the written word can sometimes be very effective in motivating people. But the spoken word is by far the most powerful form of communication between a leader and his followers. Nothing comes close to offering as wide a range of opportunities for a leader to inspire his followers, or to learn what is on their minds, as does direct oral communication. Any leader who thinks that a memo is as effective as a face-to-face meeting, or that an e-mail is as effective as a phone call, is still playing in the minor leagues.

There's a reason for this: humans have been communicating orally for hundreds of thousands of years, while the widespread use of the written word as a means of timely communication is only a few hundred years old. The contrarian leader knows that the human brain is prewired at the deepest levels in favor of the spoken word; if you wish to really inspire your followers and touch them at their emotional core, you must speak to them.

But whether dealing in oral or written communications, practically all effective leaders are to a large extent wordsmiths. In my own case I give over 150 speeches and talks each year, send out nearly two thousand individually composed letters, make close to three thousand phone calls and participate in roughly a thousand face-to-face meetings.

Words, words, words, as Hamlet would say. But getting the words right is crucial. Because as Warren Bennis has noted on so many occasions, leaders are sentenced by their sentences. So if you say or write the wrong thing at the wrong time, your *faux pas* will be propagated among your followers at warp speed, and the momentum you've worked so hard to create can be dissipated almost overnight.

But the upside potential of all these words is also enormous. Say the right things at the right time (preferably over and over) and your cause or organization can be propelled to unbelievable levels of achievement. As Mark Twain noted, "The difference between the right word and the almost right word is the difference between lightning and a lightning bug." That's one reason why a knowledge of the supertexts (discussed in Chapter 4) can be so advantageous for any leader, because the authors of the supertexts have proven to be extraordinarily successful wordsmiths.

A leader's vision is important, but finding the right words with which to express that vision and instill it in his followers' hearts is just as important. As noted in Chapter 1, much of my success as president of SUNY-Buffalo was due to my finding ways to express (and therefore unlock) the deep-seated longings of my colleagues and constituents to come out from the darkness of despair into the warm sunshine of acknowledged excellence. Similarly, my biggest challenge and most rewarding experience at USC has been finding the right words with which to motivate the Trojan Family to achieve higher levels of excellence than heretofore seemed possible.

Here we can begin to see how effective leadership almost always involves a symbiotic relationship between leader and led. If the goals and directions which the leader chooses to emphasize don't resonate with his followers, he won't be their leader for long.

So to some extent the leader must first discern the range of possibilities buried in his followers' hearts and psyches, and then choose within that range the particular goals he wishes to incorporate in his vision for the organization.

Hitler didn't single-handedly transform a pure-hearted German citizenry into war-mongering fanatics bent on world domination and genocide. Rather, he correctly sensed the potential in the hearts of his countrymen for moving in that direction, based on Germany's traditional militarism, the humiliation of the German people by the Treaty of Versailles, the despair all Germans felt as they watched the Weimer Republic and Germany's economy sink into chaos, and a strong dose of latent anti-Semitism among many Germans. Thus Hitler the master orator was able to bring to flowering among the German people a garden of evil whose seeds were already deeply planted.

Similarly, Churchill understood the willingness of the English people to stand and fight against apparently insuperable odds, while Lord Halifax, Chamberlain and the nearly traitorous Duke of Windsor did not. Churchill the master orator was able to articulate this spirit of defiance so as to stiffen the resolve of the English people beyond anything that Hitler and his generals might have imagined.

Of course, a desire on the part of a leader for a symbiotic relationship with his followers can go too far. Sometimes the leader simply abdicates his responsibility to lead and leaves all decisions concerning goals and objectives up to his followers. We can all recall political leaders in the last half-century who consistently used opinion polls as a substitute for leadership. To be sure, in a republic one would hope and expect that the opinions of the electorate over the long term would determine the policies of the national government. But the leader of that government can and should play a major role in shaping the long-term opinions of the electorate.

In the final analysis, even the strongest leaders are led to some extent by their followers. To paraphrase Machiavelli, it's perfectly all right for a leader to be manipulated by his followers, *but not too much*. The trick is to get the balance just right.

Throughout history, war has provided the most dramatic and compelling opportunity for the exercise of leadership. Moreover, war is the dominant metaphor for most areas of human endeavor in which leadership is the key to success, including business, sports, and politics; indeed, many commentators contend that business, sports, and politics are essentially *substitutes* for war. Even religious movements engage in real and metaphorical wars (jihads, the Crusades, the warrior Arjuna preparing for battle in the Bhagavad Gita, the Salvation Army, etc.), as do many benevolent causes in both the public and private sectors (the War on Poverty, the fight against cancer, the war on drugs, the battle against child pornography).

When Warren Bennis and I teach our course on leadership for upperclassmen each spring, we often ask our students on the first day of class to identify some of the most important leaders in history. Almost invariably the list includes a large number of military leaders, as well as civilians who successfully led their countries during times of war, and leaders of more peaceful pursuits who adopted a warlike approach to their endeavors. To say that war has provided the principal images and models for leadership throughout history would be an understatement.

Why should this be so? Why should war and its metaphorical surrogates play such an important role in shaping our conception of leadership? For one thing, as Churchill noted: "The story of the human race is War. Except for brief and precarious interludes, there has never been peace in the world." Moreover, war is the ultimate game, in that the penalties for losing are so terrible and painful. It's relatively easy to attract and inspire followers when their own and their families' lives, freedom and homes are on the line.

That's why so many leaders of nominally peaceful organizations try to structure their activities as a battle against the competition. Few would deny that the reason America has the best system of higher education in the world is that our universities compete intensely with one another for students, faculty, donations and research grants. This same spirit of warlike competition appears to be an important factor in building up and maintaining a successful economy.

By contrast, many observers believe that a major weakness of our public elementary and secondary schools is the fact that they are essentially geographic monopolies which aren't required to compete for students and funding. Tens of billions of dollars have been spent in support of well-intentioned efforts to reform public education in America, with relatively little to show for it. As a person who has participated over the past twenty years in many such efforts, I have to wonder whether any real reforms can ever take hold unless and until the geographic monopolies enjoyed by our public schools are broken up through the introduction of hardball competition, in which, as in an actual war, there are serious consequences for the losers.

Few people will ever play a major leadership role in a real war. But the contrarian leader understands that the metaphor of war is one of the most powerful tools he has for attracting and motivating followers. The awful feeling of being beaten or left in the dust by one's competitors, the sweet taste of victory in a tough competition for a major contract or a star faculty member or increased market share or elected office—these are the things that get followers' blood stirring, thereby making the leader's job a lot easier. Moreover, creating a sense among followers that they are under attack from outside forces, and that they must stick together and fight like hell just to survive, is the best antidote there is for combating factionalism and complacency in any organization.

One of America's Founding Fathers observed that "the surest bond of sympathy among men is mutual self-interest." And even my favorite icon of good leadership, George Washington, believed that only mutual interest, as opposed to idealism, could hold people together for very long through really tough times. From a practical standpoint, mutual interest twixt leader and led often takes the form of tangible rewards and punishments which the leader metes out to recruit and motivate followers.

The most popular medium for dispensing both rewards and punishments in the world today is money. It has been my experience that money (in the form of salary, bonuses, commissions, stock options, retirement packages, and the like) is often an essential element in attracting and retaining outstanding people, even in nonprofit and eleemosynary organizations.

However, I don't believe money is a very effective tool for *inspiring* people to reach for and achieve extraordinary goals; rather, the actual motivation in such instances seems to be pride or the desire to beat out the competition. Thus, real inspiration of followers is often brought about more by praise and exhortation from the leader than by monetary rewards alone.

That said, I must admit that I've always been fascinated by the power that money seems to have over some people. I recall participating in a corporate board meeting in which we were discussing the possibility of bringing a particular executive out of retirement to temporarily lead a troubled division. The man in question had retired three years earlier at age sixty-two with a mild heart condition. Because he and his wife had fairly modest tastes, they had already amassed more money than they would ever spend.

A colleague of mine on the board said he wasn't sure old Joe would be willing under any circumstances to take on the difficult assignment we had in mind, especially since he was enjoying his retirement so much. To which another board member responded, "Oh, don't worry, if you pay him enough he'll do it!" All the other board members laughed, stroked their chins, and nodded in agreement.

But I was stunned. Why would extra money have anything to do with old Joe's decision? I could see his agreeing to come back out of loyalty to the firm itself, or to lend a helping hand to his former colleagues; and of course, as a point of pride he would want to be paid a good salary to do so. But why would a few *additional* dollars for which he had no earthly use motivate him to endanger his health and give up something he enjoyed?

If monetary rewards have relatively little power to *inspire* (as opposed to attract and retain) followers, monetary punishments have even less. One of the great myths in American business is that stock options always tend to align the interests of management with those of the public shareholders. On the upside they probably do. But options that are "underwater" have no power either to retain or incentivize management; that's why we sometimes see boards of directors repricing or replacing underwater options so that the new option price is less than the current market price of the stock.

As noted in Chapter 6, punishments meted out by a leader are necessary for the maintenance of discipline within an organization, and under some conditions punishment can be an effective tool for the recruitment and retention of followers (e.g., the use of beatings to induce inner-city youngsters to join a gang, or Washington's insisting that ill-fed and ill-clothed deserters at Valley Forge be flogged). But as a general rule punishment is a losing strategy for leadership.

A contrarian leader of a large organization is always searching for what I like to call "leadership leverage"; that is, ways to inspire and motivate those of his followers whom he'll never come to know personally or who will never (or only rarely) hear him speak firsthand. One of the most effective means of achieving such leverage is through the establishment of multiple "people chains" through which the leader's goals, vision and values are transmitted orally and personally to every follower.

Sometimes such chains are established by design, but as often as not they simply emerge serendipitously. For example, when I give my annual address to the faculty of USC, fewer than four hundred of our twenty-five hundred full-time faculty members actually show up to hear me speak. But if I do a good job of inspiring my listeners on that particular morning, there'll be an appreciative buzz around campus by that afternoon among faculty members who weren't in attendance at my address.

Jesus was extraordinarily effective in achieving leadership leverage through people chains. He recruited a dozen principal followers, who in turn recruited hundreds of others, who in turn recruited thousands of others, and so forth to a cumulative total of billions of followers over the past two thousand years. It's important to note that the vast majority of Jesus' followers during these two millennia have been recruited through the spoken word.

One of the most important forms of leadership leverage which every leader should try to develop relates to how subordinates are treated by their supervisors throughout the leader's organization. The contrarian leader sets the tone for this process through her treatment of her chief lieutenants (see Chapter 8, "Work for Those Who Work for You"). This special group of followers then serve as leaders of their own direct reports, who in turn serve as leaders of their direct reports, and so on. The challenge is for the person at the top to be such an excellent supervisor—fair, supportive, demanding, a good listener, motivating, and inspiring—that these values will be internalized and replicated via people chains at every level in the organization. Achieving this laudable goal is very difficult, but well worth the effort, because many studies have shown that the most important single factor in employee satisfaction is the quality of the supervisor.

In examining the relationship between leaders and followers, one must always keep in mind that a given follower will have several leaders to whom he is partially loyal and by each of whom he is motivated to a greater or lesser extent. A particular follower's stable of leaders might include his immediate supervisor at work, the CEO of the company which employs him, his wife, his parish priest, the pope, the president of the United States, the commander of the National Guard unit of which he is a member, and the director of the soccer league in which he is a coach. If you are one of that person's leaders, you are necessarily competing with all the other leaders in his life for his time and attention. And that means that you (or your subordinates) must know something about that particular follower as an individual if you hope to beat out the other leaders with whom you are competing.

Therein lies a great contrarian principle: followers, be they soldiers, assembly-line workers, faculty members or voters, are not standardized units, to be counted as so many widgets on a shelf. Rather, each is a unique human being who must be recognized and treated as such if the organization or movement you're leading is to flourish over the long haul. You as the top leader may not be in a position to provide this kind of individual attention yourself to each of your followers, but it's essential that someone in your organization does so. Otherwise your ability to motivate your followers will surely erode over time.

Leaders don't really *run* organizations (although we often use that term in describing leadership). Rather, leaders lead individual followers, who collectively give motion and substance to the organization of which the leader is the head. The contrarian leader never loses sight of this fact, which is often a major reason for his success.

Chapter 10

Being President
Versus Doing President

One of the shrewdest and most contrarian insights about leadership I ever heard came from a man who—although outstanding in his academic field—wanted nothing to do with being a leader himself.

In the spring of 1970, when I was twenty-nine, I learned I had won a fellowship from the American Council on Education which would allow me to serve an administrative internship with Purdue University President Fred Hovde for the 1970–71 academic year. I was elated by the opportunity. Despite having only recently been awarded tenure and promoted to associate professor of electrical engineering at Purdue, I was already leaning toward a career in administration. With the ACE fellowship, I would be able to spend a considerable amount of time learning about university governance without having to give up my research grants or my graduate students.

Soon after the award was announced, I happened to bump into a colleague, Vern Newhouse, who was a highly respected senior member of the electrical engineering faculty.

"So, Sample," Newhouse said, "I see you've won some sort of administrative fellowship in the president's office."

"Yes, that's true," I said.

"And you'll be learning how to become an administrator?"

"I suppose so."

"And then you'll probably want to be president of a university somewhere down the road?"

"Well, I don't know. I guess I've thought about it now and then," I said, somewhat disingenuously.

He smiled and said, "Personally, I've never had any ambition whatsoever to be an administrator. I am totally inept at managing things. Why, as you may know, I can't even manage my secretary or my graduate students. But I've been a careful observer of ambitious men all my life. And here, for what it's worth, is what I've learned: many men want to *be* president, but very few want to *do* president." And with that he wished me well and walked away.

My experience over the last thirty years tells me that Professor Newhouse was absolutely right. Some of the unhappiest people I know are those whose aspirations for a high-level leadership position were finally satisfied, and who only then found out that they didn't really want to do what it is that the position required. They had spent years clawing and scraping their way up the mountain, and upon reaching their goal discovered that the realities of life at the top were a far cry from what they had imagined them to be.

Because I've been a university president for nearly twenty years, I'm often called upon to provide career counseling for people who aspire to similar positions. My advice is usually both encouraging and cautionary. On the positive side, I tell them that being the leader of a large and complex academic institution is the most enjoyable and rewarding job I've ever had or could ever imagine having. But I also share the Vern Newhouse story with them, noting that my profession is overflowing with unhappy people who worked assiduously and made enormous sacrifices to become presidents of prestigious universities, simply because they believed that was what they were *supposed* to do, and in the process gave up their chance to do what it was they really wanted to do and were really good at.

Leadership is a peculiar kind of calling. Major leadership roles, particularly at the level of a chief executive, aren't necessarily appropriate for those who have achieved distinction in positions which may be, in a hierarchical sense, lower on the totem pole. Nor should such persons, however gifted they may be, necessarily *want* to take on positions of leadership in the institutions of which they are a part. The best physician won't necessarily make a good hospital administrator or medical dean, the best engineer won't necessarily make a good division president, the best teacher won't necessarily make a good school principal, and the best athlete won't necessarily make a good coach. There is no shame, and often much merit, in a person's simply deciding he's not cut out to have power and authority over, and responsibility for, a large number of followers.

Many people aren't aware of the fact that leaders must frequently subordinate the things which they're most interested in, or which they feel are most important, to the urgent (but often ephemeral) and sometimes trivial demands of others. These others may include lieutenants, the media, politicians, protesters, board members, customers, employees, financial analysts, faculty committees and organizers of black-tie dinners. As I always tell those who aspire to academic leadership, "Along with helping to guide and shape one of the most noble and important institutions in society, a university president must also kiss a lot of frogs!"

In this regard I have come up with Sample's 70/30 Formula for Leadership—to wit, under ideal conditions up to 30 percent of a leader's time can be spent on really substantive matters, and no more than 70 percent of his time should be spent reacting to or presiding over trivial, routine or ephemeral matters. Freshman CEOs often enter the fray determined to spend most of their time as true leaders (i.e., working on issues that really count) while delegating all the trivial parts of their job to staff. Such naïfs are generally gone in a year or two, victims of a dragon born of minutiae which could have been easily slain in its infancy, but which suddenly grew to man-eating proportions. In other words, most of a top leader's time must necessarily be spent dealing with trivia and ephemera if he wants to survive and maintain his effectiveness as a leader over the long haul.

The real danger implicit in Sample's 70/30 Formula is that the 30 percent of a leader's effort devoted to important matters (such as independent thinking and inspiring his followers) may shrink to 20 percent, and then to 10 percent, and then to 5 percent, and finally to nothing, as the press of trivial and routine matters ultimately consumes all of his time and energy. I know scores of corporate CEOs and university presidents who find themselves in this position, and who feel impotent and unhappy as a result. It requires enormous discipline for the top leader in an organization to maintain the substantive component of his job near the 30 percent level.

Of course, there is no bright line separating substance from trivia and ephemera. Moreover, an activity which appears to be trivial or routine at the outset frequently turns out to be substantive, and vice versa. But on balance, Sample's 70/30 Formula provides a practical upper limit on the fraction of a leader's time and effort which can be spent on really important matters.

Thus the person who wants to *do* president (as opposed to simply *be* president) should be delighted with a 70/30 split in favor of trivia over substance. By contrast, people who need a higher percentage of substance in their lives should stay away from top leadership positions.

The news media are a challenging reality in the life of most leaders, at least in those countries fortunate enough to have a free press. The question is, how can a leader get the media to accurately present his side of the story, especially if (as is so often the case) the media's preconceived ideas about the story are negative with respect to the leader's organization or the leader himself?

Let's face it, it's extremely rare for an investigative reporter from a major newspaper to call you up and ask you how you happened to be so successful during the preceding quarter, or what it is you feel you need from the city and county governments in order to add a thousand jobs to your workforce, or how you enjoyed your much-deserved vacation. More commonly the reporter wants to know whether you have anything to say before he publishes a story the next morning based on anonymous allegations of illegal behavior on your or your company's part, or why it is that your most recent quarterly profits are below what you had projected. Readers are much more interested in bad news and scandals than they are in good news and spectacular achievements.

A contrarian leader often takes a prophylactic approach to minimizing the negative impact of the media. He spends considerable time getting to know key publishers, editors and reporters on a personal basis before a bad-news story about his organization is on the front page. He *never, ever* lies to the media, although he might very well refuse to respond to all their questions or satisfy all their demands for information.

A contrarian leader feels free to complain to the appropriate editor or reporter when a story about the leader's organization is obviously in error or grossly slanted, but he grins and bears it if the story is approximately true and even remotely evenhanded. Being able to take a public whipping from the media when you deserve it, and to do so without whining, gives you more credibility when you subsequently complain about coverage which is patently unfair.

In addition to trying to minimize bad news, the contrarian leader works hard at the much more difficult task of getting the media to carry good or even inspiring stories about his organization. Most media people are confirmed cynics; thus a major challenge for the leader is to get reporters and editors to trust him and his motives. In addition, it's often possible to win over news people by giving them advance access to stories which will interest their readers and, as a consequence, please their bosses.

USC's biggest triumph in the area of positive news coverage occurred in the fall of 1999 when we were selected as *Time* magazine's and the *Princeton Review*'s "College of the Year 2000." I remember receiving a phone call that August from a senior editor of *Time*, who said, "You know, Dr. Sample, we've had one of our best investigative reporters on your campus for the last three weeks." I said, "Yes, I'm aware of that, and frankly it's made us a little nervous." And then she said, "I'm calling to tell you that, as a result of our investigation, we've selected USC to be our College of the Year 2000!"

When the issue came out, we ordered 300,000 reprints of the article—reputedly the largest reprint order in the history of *Time* magazine—and within two weeks we had to place another order for an additional quarter million copies. Today we still get requests for reprints. The joke around campus is that every living Trojan in the world has received at least two copies, and every deceased Trojan at least one.

As you might expect, I was pretty excited about this recognition when it was first announced. In fact a couple of weeks after the announcement was made, Malcolm Currie, the former chairman of Hughes Aircraft who was then chairman of USC's board of trustees, had one of the reprints cut apart, had each page laminated in plastic, and then had the pages rebound with a small spiral binder. He presented it to me at a board of trustees meeting and said, "Here, Steve, now you can take the damned thing into the shower with you and read it every morning!"

A really talented leader can even use a hostile press to get his story out to followers and supporters. The two most gifted practitioners of this rare art in American history were Franklin Roosevelt and Ronald Reagan. Their situations were quite different: FDR was a liberal who faced a largely conservative press, and Reagan a conservative who faced a largely liberal press. But both men were able to speak through the media to their countrymen. And no matter how hard the press might have tried to distort their messages, somehow these two presidents were able to consistently connect with the American people.

An effective contrarian tool for garnering both media attention and the attention of the public at large is what I like to call "counterintuitive hooks"—short, one-sentence statements which sound patently false but which are in fact absolutely true. As was pointed out in Chapter 1, most people are binary in their thinking—they feel compelled to immediately classify everything they hear as either true or false. Consequently, when they hear a counterintuitive hook, they can't get it out of their mind—it just won't stay put in either the "true" or the "not true" box in their brain.

A simple example will illustrate the concept of a counterintuitive hook. Shortly after I became president of USC I was working with a colleague on an outline for an upcoming speech. The draft she had given me included the line, "USC is one of the largest private employers in Los Angeles." I circled this line and said, "We need something more quantitative here."

"Like what?" she asked.

"Well, like 'USC is one of the ten largest private employers in L.A.'"

"But Steve, I'm sure we're not one of the ten largest."

"OK," I said, "Then we're one of the fifteen largest, or twenty largest, or whatever. Just find out what our rank really is, and we'll put it in the speech so our listeners will have a quantitative takeaway."

The next day she came to me and said, "Steve, you won't believe this, but USC is far and away the largest private employer in the whole city of Los Angeles."

"Martha, are you *sure?*"

"Absolutely," she said, and showed me the hard data.

"Well," I said, "The data are incontrovertible. But in my heart I don't believe it, and neither will my audience."

"So then, we should take it out?" she asked.

"Oh, no," I replied, "Leave it in. It will stick in the minds of all who hear it. They'll know intuitively that it simply can't be true that USC is the largest private employer in L.A.; they'll be certain that that accolade belongs to an aerospace firm or a movie studio or a bank or some other company inside the city limits. But they'll also figure that the president of USC is not a liar and that he probably did his homework before making such an outrageous statement. Because most people are uncomfortable with ambiguity, this little puppy will bounce back and forth in their brains for a long time between 'true' and 'not true.' And when they finally learn that our hook is absolutely true in every respect, they will be left with a lasting positive impression of USC."

Indeed, that's exactly what happened. Scores of people from around the country challenged the idea that a university could be the largest private employer in the second-largest city in the United States. Hundreds of others simply didn't believe it. Even the media treated this counterintuitive hook with great care and skepticism—e.g., "USC claims to be the largest private employer in Los Angeles," or "It is alleged that . . ."

Then suddenly this particular hook became a universally accepted fact. People by the dozens would come up to me and say, "Steve, did you know that USC is the largest private employer in Los Angeles?" Newspapers printed it as a simple declarative sentence, as though all their readers already knew it. During the 2001 NCAA men's basketball tournament I heard it cited by sports announcers on national television as a well-known fact about Los Angeles.

From a more practical standpoint, this counterintuitive hook began to elevate USC in the eyes of donors, politicians, business leaders and other influential people. They sensed (correctly, I believe) that fifteen or twenty years ago USC would not have been L.A.'s largest private employer, and that the university had moved into the number one spot, not by virtue of its own growth, but by the demise or flight of other large employers which theretofore had been located within the city limits. Thus, as these leaders discovered that USC was L.A.'s last remaining large employer in the private sector, they developed a more protective and supportive attitude toward the university.

There are innumerable ways in which a leader can use counterintuitive hooks to the advantage of his organization or movement. A few others that have been helpful to USC and our eponymous region are:

- USC, located in the center of Los Angeles, enjoys a substantially lower crime rate than either Stanford or Harvard.
- Higher education in Southern California is a larger industry than aerospace.
- The world center of the biomedical technology industry is Southern, not Northern, California.

The key is that each such counterintuitive hook must be absolutely true. A hook which is an exaggeration, or which cannot be readily verified with hard data, can backfire in very unpleasant and counterproductive ways.

When I was a junior in high school one of my teachers said to me, "Steve, you are by nature a perfectionist; you never know when to stop trying to make a thing better. So here's something for you to keep in mind: Anything worth doing at all is worth doing poorly. It may be worth more if it's done well, but it's worth something if it's done poorly."

Now there is contrarian advice with a vengeance! When I first heard it I thought my teacher was an idiot. But since then, as I've had to live with my inborn perfectionism for forty-five additional years, I've come to see that my teacher wasn't as stupid as I thought he was.

Conventional wisdom talks incessantly about the pursuit of excellence at any cost, about leaving no stone unturned in an unrelenting quest for the highest possible quality, about sparing no expense in order to achieve perfection, and so forth. Such maxims may make good sense for followers and managers, especially if they happen to be naturally inclined toward sloppiness and second-rate performance. But the very notion of perfection is almost antithetical to effective leadership.

As has been pointed out several times in earlier chapters, leaders in the real world are almost always forced to make trade-offs among competing priorities. If, in quest of perfection, a leader is willing to allow one of these priorities to have unlimited access to the limited resources (e.g., time, space, money, people) available to him, all the other priorities will surely suffer and the leader's organization will almost surely fail.

Whatever it is you're doing can always be done better, and hence there is no upper bound on the amount of resources that can be consumed in the pursuit of perfection. Thus the contrarian leader's maxim in this arena is: *Anything worth doing at all is worth doing just well enough*. The tricky job for the leader is deciding what "just well enough" means in each particular situation.

When General Patton was chasing the German army across Europe in 1945 and found his way blocked by a destroyed bridge across a major river, he wasn't interested in building a new bridge that met the highest standards of excellence; he wasn't even interested in building the world's greatest temporary bridge. All he wanted was a bridge that was *just good enough* to allow his tanks and troops to cross the river, and to cross it only once.

The same sort of principle applies to product development in competitive industries. The corporate graveyard is full of defunct companies that literally spared no expense in perfecting their product, and then found there were no customers willing to pay the price which such a perfect product required in order to be economically viable. By contrast, successful companies are smart enough to quit chasing product perfection when the incremental cost of further improvements exceeds what people are willing to pay, or, equivalently, when such further improvements are not all that beneficial to the end user.

Warren Bennis once told me that he was an example of a person with an excellent personal radar; such people are extremely sensitive to the thoughts, feelings and wishes of others, and as a consequence are constantly turning their attention from one thing or person to another, and then another, and then another. Bennis added that he thought I was an example of a person with a good internal gyrocompass; such people can stay steadily on course no matter how many distractions may impinge on them from every side.

The problem is that neither a good personal radar nor a good internal gyrocompass is sufficient to make a person an effective leader. The radar-equipped find it hard to stay on course long enough to get anything accomplished, while the gyro-equipped are liable to run into an iceberg at full steam.

The contrarian leader knows he should have both. And if he's not blessed with both from birth (and practically no one is), he knows he must either develop an artificial radar (or an artificial gyrocompass, as the case may be), or recruit a lieutenant who has the particular property which the leader lacks.

Here we might draw a parallel to Machiavelli's dictum that it is best for a leader to be both feared and loved, but if he must make an exclusive choice between the two he should prefer to be feared. Similarly, if a leader must choose between being sensitive to others and being able to stay on course, he should prefer the latter.

A close cousin of this last principle is attributable to President Franklin Roosevelt, who said that "energy is more efficient than efficiency." No matter how sophisticated a potential leader may be in thinking free, artful listening and making decisions, the contrarian knows that drive and enthusiasm have a lot to do with determining who wins and who loses at the end of the day. In his book *Being Lucky*, Herman Wells, the famous mid-twentieth-century president of Indiana University, made essentially this same point. It helps to be smart and creative, Wells noted, but the two most important ingredients for successful leadership are energy and luck.

Finally, no organization can survive in the long term if its leader eschews all change in an effort to preserve the status quo. As noted earlier, the essence of leadership is motivating followers to change, and this is true even for conservative organizations and movements. As G. K. Chesterton once said:

> Conservatism is based upon the idea that if you leave things alone you leave them as they are. But you do not. If you leave a thing alone you leave it to a torrent of changes.

If you leave a white post alone it will soon be a black post. If you particularly want it to be white you must be always painting it again; that is, you must be always having a revolution. Briefly, if you want the old white post you must have a new white post.

When a person first attains a top leadership position, he's often dazzled by the perquisites and deferential treatment which accompany high office; indeed, these may well be the things that motivated him to seek the top job in the first place. But soon these ephemeral glories fade and he's left with the realities of his job—the nitty-gritty of day-to-day leadership. It's then that Vern Newhouse's insight, cited at the beginning of this chapter, comes into play. Does this person want simply to *be* president, or does he really want to *do* president? If the latter, he might contribute something great and lasting to his followers and the organization they comprise. But if he only wants to *be* president, the sooner he's removed from office the better for everyone concerned, including the leader himself.

Chapter 11

The University of Southern California: A Case Study in Contrarian Leadership

I should like to turn now to an explicit example of contrarian leadership in action: the evolution of the University of Southern California over the decade from 1991 to 2001. Many observers feel that this institution has made greater gains academically in this ten-year period than any other university in the country. I don't know whether that superlative is true, but certainly USC has come a long way in a relatively short time, and its progress has been driven in large part by a number of contrarian decisions that were made during that period.

It should be noted at the outset that the changes and achievements I'm about to relate are not due primarily to my efforts. The lion's share of the credit belongs to my brilliant administrative team, scores of extremely talented and dedicated faculty members, hundreds of hardworking staff and supportive alumni, a number of very far-sighted donors, a board of trustees who provided excellent guidance and who were willing to stay the course when the going got rough, and thousands of exceptionally bright and ambitious students.

As noted in Chapter 2, I had arranged for an interregnum of nearly four months from the announcement of my appointment in early December of 1990 to my first day of work in late March of 1991. This gave me ample opportunity to think free, think gray and listen gray, hearing extensively from members of the USC community about what they felt was working and what they felt was broken. And I learned a great deal about what was in the hearts of members of the Trojan Family—their hopes and fears and their yearning to see USC become stronger academically and make a bigger impact in the world.

The decade started inauspiciously enough. For one thing, California was mired in a deep recession. Because of large shortfalls in tuition revenue, USC was forced to make major layoffs late in 1991—the first in our history. The decision to reduce our employee base by 8 percent was extremely difficult and painful. In the process we eliminated eight hundred positions, five hundred of which were still occupied by real flesh-and-blood human beings.

Of course, many profit-seeking companies undergo substantial staff reductions as a matter of routine—almost like a periodic purgative. But universities are different: a massive layoff such as we implemented is extremely rare in higher education, and under certain conditions can be highly destabilizing. Nonetheless, given the extraordinary budget difficulties we faced in 1991, the phasing out of eight hundred jobs at USC was absolutely necessary to restore the university to financial health. In keeping with contrarian wisdom we implemented the entire set of cuts all at once, rather than string them out over several years.

To further complicate our efforts at reform and innovation we had to live through the devastating riots of 1992, followed by the Northridge earthquake which severely damaged much of the infrastructure and a great deal of private property in Los Angeles County. But once we got all of this bad news behind us, the fortunes of USC became extraordinarily positive—beyond our most optimistic hopes and dreams. The question is: Why did these good things happen?

A very important first step which we took early on in the decade was to create a role and mission statement that was at a slant to the mission statements of many peer universities (see Exhibit 1). This project had its origins in an off-the-cuff request from a trustee at a board meeting: "Steve," he asked, "would you please write down all the things that make USC similar to other leading research universities, and all the things that make us different from every other university, and get it all to fit on one letter-size page in 12-point type?"

It was the one-page requirement that transformed this trustee's innocent request into a very formidable undertaking. I spent at least a hundred hours working on this project. I sent draft after draft out to faculty and administrative colleagues and trustees, encouraging them to add to the text with impunity *provided* they indicated what words in the draft should be eliminated in order to hold the statement to one page in length.

When the final role and mission statement was adopted by the trustees in 1993, it gave our academic community a clear sense of identity and provided a solid base on which our efforts to improve the university could be anchored. Because the role and mission statement was so short, and because it articulated the core values of the institution, it was widely read and internalized and lent itself to being quoted and exegeted in hundreds of reports, letters, speeches and meetings.

Right after the role and mission statement was completed, our provost and a small committee of senior faculty began work on a strategic plan for USC. Unlike most academic plans, which often run to hundreds of pages and have dozens of priorities, ours was very contrarian in that it was extremely brief and succinct, comprising only fifteen pages (including appendices) and only four strategic priorities. As with the role and mission statement, brevity turned out to be one of the plan's greatest virtues; people actually *read* the thing and bought in to its values and directions.

The crafting of a role and mission statement and a strategic plan, in and of themselves, might appear to be among the least contrarian leadership techniques espoused in this book, as anyone who's followed the *Dilbert* cartoon strip knows. Indeed, most role and mission statements and strategic plans fully deserve the ridicule they elicit. But contrarian role and mission statements

---

EXHIBIT 1. The Role and Mission
of the University of Southern California.

The central mission of the university of Southern California is
the development of human beings and society as a whole through
the cultivation and enrichment of the human mind and spirit.
The principal means by which our mission is accomplished are
teaching, research, artistic creation, professional practice and
selected forms of public service.

Our first priority as faculty and staff is the education of our students, from freshmen to postdoctorals, through a broad array of
academic, professional, extracurricular and athletic programs of
the first rank. The integration of liberal and professional learning
is one of USC's special strengths. We strive constantly for excellence in teaching knowledge and skills to our students, while at
the same time helping them to acquire wisdom and insight, love
of truth and beauty, moral discernment, understanding of self, and
respect and appreciation for others.

Research of the highest quality by our faculty and students is
fundamental to our mission. USC is one of a very small number
of premier academic institutions in which research and teaching
are inextricably intertwined, and on which the nation depends
for a steady stream of new knowledge, art, and technology. Our
faculty are not simply teachers of the works of others but active
contributors to what is taught, thought and practiced throughout
the world.

---

and strategic plans dispense with meaningless bromides in order
to get to the nitty-gritty—to articulate some consistent values and
strategic principles that every follower and stakeholder recognizes
as the basis for all the decisions and actions of the organization.

To use an example from the business sector, one of Jack
Welch's foremost contributions to General Electric was the artic-
ulation of a basic action plan: (1) to ensure that every business
unit at GE attained first- or second-place status against the competition and (2) that any business unit which couldn't achieve

USC is pluralistic, welcoming outstanding men and women of every race, creed and background. We are a global institution in a global center, attracting more international students over the years than any other American university. And we are private, unfettered by political control, strongly committed to academic freedom, and proud of our entrepreneurial heritage.

An extraordinary closeness and willingness to help one another are evident among USC students, alumni, faculty, and staff; indeed, for those within its compass the Trojan Family is a genuinely supportive community. Alumni, trustees, volunteers and friends of USC are essential to this family tradition, providing generous financial support, participating in university governance, and assisting students at every turn.

In our surrounding neighborhoods and around the globe, USC provides public leadership and public service in such diverse fields as health care, economic development, social welfare, scientific research, public policy and the arts. We also serve the public interest by being the largest private employer in the city of Los Angeles, as well as the city's largest export industry in the private sector.

USC has played a major role in the development of Southern California for more than a century, and plays an increasingly important role in the development of the nation and the world. We expect to continue to play these roles for many centuries to come. Thus our planning, commitments and fiscal policies are directed toward building quality and excellence in the long term.

---

such performance would be cut loose. Similarly, Miramax's success in motion pictures has resulted from a simple action formula demanding (1) low cost and (2) stories dealing compellingly with the human condition. Such clarity allows people at every level in those companies to understand what is expected of them both individually and collectively.

It was through USC's strategic plan that we articulated our overarching goal: to become in fact and by reputation one of the ten leading private research universities in America. It was also through the planning process that we came to adopt a great contrarian principle: an institution cannot copy its way to excellence; rather, true excellence can only be achieved through original thinking and unconventional approaches. Toward that end we made conscious and somewhat risky decisions to undertake strategic initiatives in undergraduate education, interdisciplinary research and teaching, internationalization, and the exploitation of our location in Los Angeles and Southern California. In the same way that reading one book precludes reading many others, we soberly chose these particular four priorities over many other viable ones, realizing that we could end up being passed by if we guessed incorrectly or if fortune ruled against us.

Our highest strategic priority was to dramatically improve every aspect of undergraduate education at our institution. While our graduate and professional programs were highly regarded around the country, USC in 1991 at the undergraduate level was viewed by many high school counselors and much of the general public as a party school in a dangerous and decaying neighborhood. This reputation was to a large extent inaccurate and undeserved. But deserved or not, our reputation had put us in a downward spiral when it came to recruiting undergraduate students. Things had become so desperate that the university was accepting applications for admission to the fall semester as late as one week into the semester itself. As a consequence, dropout rates were high and graduation rates were abysmally low.

Thus we realized that an essential part of our effort to improve undergraduate education would necessarily involve improving student selectivity. To this end we made the contrarian decision to eliminate need-blind admissions for the weaker applicants, reduce the loan component and increase the grant component of our need-based aid packages for the better applicants, inaugurate an extensive program of merit-based aid, and reduce the target size of our freshman class by 500 students relative to its historic maximum. This last was an especially counterintuitive strategy in view of our budget problems at the time.

We also made radical changes in the undergraduate curriculum. First among these changes was the development of a new six-course core curriculum which is now required of all students, from engineers to English majors. A key attraction for students is the fact that most courses in the core are taught by senior faculty in small classes. Here again one can see contrarian wisdom in action. Generating freshman and sophomore credit hours with senior faculty in small classes is one of the most inefficient and "wasteful" things a university can do; it is far cheaper to use graduate assistants to teach lower-division courses, or to teach these courses with professors lecturing to classes of a thousand students or more. Moreover, at many research universities it's difficult to find senior faculty who are willing to teach freshmen and sophomores at all. But scores of our very best tenured faculty responded enthusiastically to the challenges of the new core curriculum, with the result that freshmen and sophomores at USC now develop much closer relations with senior faculty than they would at most other research universities.

It has been conventional wisdom in American higher education for nearly a century that a student's minor should relate as closely as possible to his major—that is, if he's majoring in English literature, for example, he should minor in a closely allied field such as British history or comparative literature. This approach worked fine when the baccalaureate was the terminal degree for most students. But in America today, the vast majority of undergraduates at the better universities will go on to earn at least one advanced degree. Thus undergraduate education for the more competitive students is in fact preparatory education prior to these students' attending graduate school. Under these circumstances it makes little sense for students to pursue highly specialized curricula at the undergraduate level.

This simple fact led to our turning conventional academic wisdom on its head. We now encourage all our students to stretch themselves mentally by selecting a minor which is far removed across the intellectual landscape from their major—combining a minor in music with a major in sociology, for example, or a minor in business with a major in physics. To facilitate this approach our faculty developed over one hundred minors in a very wide range of disciplines, including minors in fields such as law or preventive medicine which are normally closed to undergraduates. We also established a Renaissance Scholars program to honor those students who are especially successful at pursuing two or more widely separated fields of study.

As noted in Chapter 8, an effective leader recruits excellent subordinates, defines success, and then helps his subordinates achieve that success. My second-in-command, provost Lloyd Armstrong, did just that in 1993 when he hired Joe Allen as our vice provost for enrollment management and director of admissions. Joe, who died tragically in 2001 at age fifty-three, proved to be a marketing and recruiting genius—in all probability the best in the country.

Finally, we greatly expanded our program of residential colleges, implemented a new BA/MD program which guarantees thirty-seven selected incoming freshmen a seat in our medical school four years hence, and developed extensive opportunities for undergraduates to engage in research with senior faculty.

The results attributable to these changes have been nothing short of spectacular. USC is now in the top 1 percent of all colleges and universities in America in terms of selectivity. Our average SAT scores—1308 for the fall 2000 freshman class—reflect an increase of 240 points, an extraordinary (and perhaps unprecedented) gain, even allowing for the national recentering of SAT scores in 1995. In addition, the average GPA of incoming students last fall was 3.9, and most of our freshmen came from the upper 5 percent of their high school graduating class. We now attract nine applications for every opening in our freshman class, and we rank in the top ten of all institutions in America in terms of the number of National Merit Scholars who matriculate as freshmen. Ironically, our location in Los Angeles has now become a major plus factor in our recruitment efforts.

USC has recently received extensive national recognition for the excellence of its undergraduate programs. As noted earlier,

Time magazine and the *Princeton Review* named us College of the Year 2000 for our community outreach efforts. In the fall of 2000 we were identified as one of America's "hottest" schools by *The Newsweek/Kaplan College Guide*. More recently, USC was designated as one of only sixteen national Leadership Institutions by the Association of American Colleges and Universities for the excellence of our undergraduate offerings.

We now compete very favorably with the entire University of California system in attracting the best students (in spite of the UC's six-to-one price advantage in tuition), and we are beginning to take outstanding students away from Stanford, Harvard, and Yale. Best of all, retention and graduation rates have improved dramatically. We've moved from a 53 percent graduation rate for the class of 1988 to a 73 percent graduation rate for the class of 1998 (the most recent figures available, since national graduation rates are calculated six years after a particular class enters the university). Our year-to-year retention figures (freshman to sophomore, sophomore to junior, etc.) have been 95 percent or better, which promises to yield graduation rates above 80 percent in the near future.

When we began our efforts in 1991 to overhaul undergraduate education, we knew that eventually we would have to compete head-to-head with any and all of the Ivy League schools. The following quote from a letter I recently received from a USC alum reflects the progress we've made to date:

A longtime friend and accomplished television and film producer approached me the other day to compliment USC. He reminded me that he had been, for over twenty years, a senior West Coast recruiting alumnus for Yale University. 2001 was the first year in Yale's history that the university lost nearly a dozen potential students to USC. These students who chose to become members of the Trojan Family were not bought by scholarships. These students had the strength of both their academic and extracurricular activities to be admitted to Yale, but chose at their own discretion to attend USC this fall. So great was the loss to Yale that a special meeting was held among the senior recruitment staff at the university to discuss how better to market Yale to top students so as to prevent this circumstance from reoccurring. My friend said to me, "You should be very, very proud of this accomplishment. Why are you not acting elated?" I responded by saying, whereas I am overjoyed, I am certainly not surprised.

The second major achievement of the past decade has been a substantial strengthening of USC's research mission. Three key contrarian strategies have been responsible for much of this improvement. First was the realization that postdoctoral education was quickly replacing doctoral education as the terminal academic credential in the natural sciences, psychology and selected fields of engineering. Thus, in advance of most other universities, USC realized that postdoctoral education would be an increasingly important factor in determining both the quality and quantity of sponsored research at leading research universities.

The second and third contrarian strategies we pursued with respect to research were to emphasize interdisciplinary projects, and to exploit our location in Los Angeles and Southern California. Often these two strategies were combined, as in the Integrated Media Systems Center, a national center of excellence in multimedia technologies funded by a $16 million grant from the National Science Foundation and $33 million in industrial and other matching funds; and the Institute for Creative Technologies, a national center of excellence in computer simulation and virtual reality funded by a $45 million contract from the Department of the Army. Both of these projects are highly interdisciplinary, and both take advantage of USC's location in Los Angeles and Southern California.

Indeed, Southern California has a number of characteristics which have proven to be especially helpful in growing USC's sponsored research base. First, for better or worse this region has become the urban paradigm for the twenty-first century, repre-senting as it does a coming together of the world's people unmatched in human history. Then too, Los Angeles has emerged as the de facto capital city of the Pacific Rim. And the fact that Southern California is the locus of the motion picture and tele-vision industries has made this area the world center of excellence for combining technology with creative content. Finally, as men-tioned briefly in Chapter 9, Southern California is now the world center of the biomedical technology industry.

As a result of the foregoing contrarian and opportunistic strategies, our sponsored research has nearly doubled over the past decade to $325 million a year. USC now ranks among the top ten of all private universities in terms of the dollar volume of federal research support, ahead of such worthy private competitors as Duke, Chicago, and Caltech and such worthy public competitors as Berkeley and North Carolina.

Another measure of the academic strength of any university is the number of faculty who have been elected to membership in the three national academies—the National Academy of Engi-neering, the National Academy of Sciences, and the Institute of Medicine. At USC that number has nearly doubled over the past ten years to a total of forty, thanks in part to a concerted effort to make certain that outstanding faculty at USC are given full and fair consideration for election to these prestigious organizations.

Our researchers are getting more media attention, not only in science and medicine, but in law and the social sciences as well. We've also seen a significant increase in media coverage of our poets, novelists, musicians, artists, and architects. In addition to gratifying current faculty members, this increased publicity makes it easier for us to recruit outstanding professors from other insti-tutions. In this regard, nothing generated more favorable atten-tion for our university in the worldwide academic community than the awarding of the undivided Nobel Prize in Chemistry in 1994 to our own Professor George Olah for work that he did over the last twenty years at USC.

Our third major achievement of the past ten years has been the development of new disciplinary and interdisciplinary strengths at USC. Of course, many of our traditional schools, departments and programs were already strong in 1991, and are still strong today. But several others have achieved real national prominence during the last decade, often due to the application of contrarian principles.

First among these improved programs is the Keck School of Medicine at USC. The school has made phenomenal progress in the last ten years. We can see this progress in the extraordinary success of our hospital partners, the dramatic increase in the faculty's clinical practice, and the huge growth in sponsored research in medicine. These achievements were recognized in 1999 when the W. M. Keck Foundation awarded a $110 million naming gift to our medical school.

A contrarian principle that has played an important role in advancing our medical school has been our continuing commitment to *not* owning and operating our major teaching hospitals. Prior to the 1990s, most people believed that, with the exception of Harvard, a university medical school which did not own its own teaching hospitals was doomed to second-rate status. But exactly the opposite has proven to be the case in so many instances that USC is now seen as being prescient in this regard.

The entire field of communications at USC has also advanced dramatically in the past ten years, especially through the contrarian approach of bringing together a number of putatively disparate parts—namely, the Annenberg School for Communication, the School of Cinema-Television, the School of Journalism, and many programs in the School of Engineering, including the Information Sciences Institute, the Integrated Media Systems Center, and the Institute for Creative Technologies. The pivotal event that triggered this coming together was Walter and Lee Annenberg's $120 million cash gift in 1993 to establish the Annenberg Center for Communication. Thanks to the Annenbergs, USC's programs in communication, taken as a whole, are now the strongest of any American university.

The arts have also emerged as a great strength of the university. USC has five professional schools in the arts—Cinema-Television, the Thornton School of Music, Theatre, Architecture, and Fine Arts. Some of these were already quite strong ten years ago. But today, taken together, we believe these five schools and their joint programs constitute the strongest offering in the arts of any university in the United States.

Several other units at USC have achieved national stature over the last ten years, including the Marshall School of Business, physical therapy, computer science, computational genomics, environmental marine biology and creative writing. The point is this: we've maintained our lead in fields where we were already strong, while moving up considerably in a number of other disciplines. This is one of the keys to building a great university over the long haul.

USC's fourth major achievement over the past decade has been fundraising. More than needing new buildings, we desperately needed to increase our endowment. Conventional wisdom held that we should set rather modest fundraising goals for ourselves, given the effects of Southern California's recession on many of our alumni, and the widespread belief that philanthropists are more interested in naming buildings than in supporting academic programs through gifts to endowment. But our contrarian instincts convinced us that we could in fact raise large sums for endowment, and that we should cast our fundraising net not only among our own alumni, but also among non-alums who were close to the university, and even among people who had no affinity with USC whatsoever.

We began our Building on Excellence campaign with a goal of raising $1 billion in new gifts and pledges in the seven years from 1993 to 2000. We surpassed that billion-dollar goal early in

1998, then raised the goal to $1.5 billion, surpassed that new goal in late 1999, and finally raised the goal to $2 billion and extended the duration of the campaign through 2002.

Our campaign total to date (mid-2001) is $1.9 billion. When we're finished next year this campaign will stand as the third most successful in the history of American higher education, just behind the most recent campaigns of Columbia and Harvard.

During the past decade we have nearly *quintupled* our endowment, from $440 million in 1990 to just under $2.2 billion in 2000. A good part of this growth has been due to shrewd investing in an unprecedented bull market, but much of it can be attributed to new donations as well. In the past seven years we have received three gifts of more than $100 million each—from the Annenbergs, Alfred Mann, and the Keck Foundation; these gifts in and of themselves have set a new record in college and university fundraising. It should be pointed out that all three of these megagifts came from non-alumni or foundations headed by non-alumni; moreover, all three were for endowment, not bricks and mortar.

We've been fortunate to receive naming gifts as a part of this campaign for five of our professional schools—the Leventhal School of Accounting, the Marshall School of Business, the Rossier School of Education, the Thornton School of Music and the Keck School of Medicine. Each of these naming gifts was, at the time it was given, the largest gift in history to a school of that kind. Endowed chairs and professorships have grown from 152 at the beginning of the campaign to 253 today—an increase of almost 67 percent. Annual alumni giving has gone from an 11 percent participation rate to 34 percent, and in all probability we'll reach our goal of a 37 percent annual participation rate by 2002.

What were the contrarian keys to the success of this campaign? First was our ability to persuade donors to make large endowment gifts in support of specific programs, rather than focusing primarily on buildings; second, our widespread use of outstanding faculty and students as part of the donor-cultivation process; and third, our ability to tap sources of support far removed from our alumni base while still capitalizing on the deep affection that practically all members of the Trojan Family have for USC.

From the moment my appointment as president of USC was first announced in December of 1990, I was urged by countless numbers of people to begin the process of moving USC out of Los Angeles. These people sincerely believed that L.A. as a viable urban center was dead as a doornail, and that the only way USC could survive and thrive was to move to either Malibu (as Pepperdine University had done a few years before) or to Orange County.

The trustees, however, adopted a contrarian approach. Rather than view Los Angeles and our surrounding community as major liabilities, they urged my colleagues and me to find ways to transform our current location into a major positive factor in the life of the university.

For starters, we decided USC should make visible and sustained improvements in the neighborhoods surrounding both the University Park campus and the Health Sciences campus. We began this process with three contrarian principles in mind. First, we wanted to narrow the focus of our public service programs and concentrate on our immediate neighborhoods, in order to make a dramatic difference in the physical appearance and quality of life in those neighborhoods. Second, we wanted to form respectful partnerships and real collaborations with our neighbors, as opposed to taking a *noblesse oblige* approach. And third, we were determined not to engage in "urban removal"—that is, no seizing of property through condemnation and no bulldozing people out of their homes.

What kinds of programs have evolved through this effort? One particularly noteworthy example is our Good Neighbors campaign. In 1990 we were raising about $100,000 a year from faculty and staff contributions to the United Way. Today, through the

Good Neighbors campaign, we are raising nearly $650,000 a year through voluntary contributions from faculty and staff. Every penny of this money is invested in neighborhood projects, each of which is a joint venture between a community-based organization and a campus-based group.

We now have very close ties to our Family of Five Schools, which comprises the five public schools nearest to our University Park campus, and we've entered into close partnerships with two additional schools near the Health Sciences campus. Three of these seven schools have been designated as California Distinguished Schools, which means they are among the best public schools in the state.

We've instituted a very successful program of community-based policing, which includes KidWatch, a program that involves seven hundred of our neighbors who volunteer to watch out for the children in our neighborhood as they go to and from school. We offer a bonus of $25,000 to any employee who wishes to own and occupy housing close to one of our two campuses. And our Business Expansion Network is one of the most successful in the state; as a result, dozens of small businesses have been started and are thriving in our neighborhoods.

We've dramatically increased student, faculty, and staff participation in community outreach programs. Nearly ten thousand of our fifteen thousand undergraduates engage in substantial community service every year; we believe that's the best record of any college or university in the country. As a side benefit, this culture of public service among our undergraduates has proven to be a major attraction to excellent students from around the country.

Our community service efforts have also attracted a great deal of private investment in our neighborhoods. Along the way we've received wide national recognition for these efforts, which in turn has helped us in fundraising and in competition for research grants. Out of all this we have deduced a great contrarian truth: *If you want to transform a troubled neighborhood, start with safe streets and good public schools; the rest will follow.*

Looking back it's been an exhilarating ten-year ride, not just for me as president, but for everyone associated with USC. Hundreds of people have had an opportunity to develop and demonstrate their leadership skills. Contrarian principles—from artful listening, to thinking gray and free, to going against conventional wisdom—have been evident at every turn. Along the way we've made lots of mistakes and had to backtrack numerous times, but those missteps haven't dampened people's enthusiasm for the overarching goal.

In the final analysis it's deeply satisfying to be involved in a project which transcends any one individual, and which will serve the best interests of society as a whole for centuries to come. Indeed, that's the best reason I can think of for *doing* president.

Conclusion

I began this study of contrarian leadership by pointing out there is no infallible step-by-step formula for becoming an effective leader, and certainly not for becoming a *good* leader. But we can at least pull together a few contrarian principles which will help a leader break free of the wisdom of the herd, and strike out in bold new directions:

1. Think gray: try not to form firm opinions about ideas or people unless and until you have to.
2. Think free: train yourself to move several steps beyond traditional brainstorming by considering really outrageous solutions and approaches.
3. Listen first, talk later; and when you listen, do so artfully.
4. Experts can be helpful, but they're no substitute for your own critical thinking and discernment.
5. Beware of pseudoscience masquerading as incontrovertible fact or unassailable wisdom; it typically will do nothing to serve your interests or those of the organization you are leading.
6. Dig for gold in the supertexts while your competition stays mired down in trade publications and other ephemera; you

can depend on your lieutenants to give you any current news that really matters.

7. Never make a decision yourself that can reasonably be delegated to a lieutenant; and never make a decision today that can reasonably be put off to tomorrow.

8. Ignore sunk costs and yesterday's mistakes; the decisions you make as a leader can only affect the future, not the past.

9. Don't unnecessarily humiliate a defeated opponent.

10. Know which hill you're willing to die on, and realize that your choice may at some point require you to retreat from all the surrounding hills.

11. Work for those who work for you; recruit the best lieutenants available, and then spend most of your time and energy helping them to succeed.

12. Many people want to *be* leader, but few want to *do* leader; if you're not in the latter group you should stay away from the leader business altogether.

13. You as a leader can't really run your organization; rather, you can only lead individual followers, who then collectively give motion and substance to the organization of which you are the head.

14. Don't delude yourself into thinking that people are intrinsically better or worse than they really are; instead, work to bring out the best in your followers (and yourself) while minimizing the worst.

15. You can't copy your way to excellence; rather, true excellence can only be achieved through original thinking and unconventional approaches.

All of the foregoing principles are predicated on an underlying belief that leadership is highly situational and contingent; as noted earlier, what works in one context at one point in time won't necessarily work in a different context at the same time, or in the same context at a different time. Thus, every leader is locked in a moment-to-moment struggle with the context and circumstances of his own place and time, which raises the question of whether he can ever truly hope to be the master of that struggle. This conundrum in turn causes us to wonder whether leaders are the architects of history, or history is the architect of leaders.

In the course on leadership that Warren Bennis and I teach at USC, we contrast the views of Leo Tolstoy, who believed that history shapes and determines leaders, with those of Thomas Carlyle, who believed that leaders shape and determine history. In his epilogue to perhaps the greatest of all novels, *War and Peace,* Tolstoy argued that kings and generals are history's slaves. That is, Tolstoy believed that leaders merely ride the crests of historical waves which have been set in motion by myriad forces beyond these leaders' control or comprehension. "Every act of theirs, which appears to them an act of their own free will," he wrote, "is in an historical sense involuntary and is related to the whole cause of history and predestined from eternity."

On the other side is Carlyle, the nineteenth-century British historian and essayist, who was convinced that "history is the biography of great men," the greatest of them being kings. The very word *king,* Carlyle contends, derives from the ancient word *can-ning,* which means "able man." In Carlyle's view, it is the Ablemen (and Ablewomen) of our species who direct the course of history and determine humanity's destiny.

My experiences as a leader, as well as my study of chaos theory and related phenomena, have led me to a middle ground between Tolstoy and Carlyle. It may well be that our world is largely Tolstoyan, subject to historical forces which no man or woman can fully measure and analyze, and the consequences of which no person can fully predict. Thus, to that extent, leaders are in fact history's slaves. However, I am also convinced that Ablemen and Ablewomen *can* make a difference in the course of human events; that the decisions of leaders can indeed have a lasting impact on the world; that historical determinism is never totally in control.

The exquisite part of all this is that a given leader at a given moment never knows for sure whether he is acting as an architect of history or simply as history's pawn. If he's like most human beings he wants desperately to believe the former. And contrarian wisdom would argue that that is the morally preferable approach: *A leader should always act as though he himself, not history or fate, is responsible for his actions.*

A closely related theme in this book is that contrarian leaders should assiduously cultivate and jealously guard their intellectual independence. Warren Bennis has famously observed that "managers do things right, while leaders do the right thing." But what is the right thing? In countless leadership scenarios that play out in a pluralistic society, no two people will agree.

The contrarian leader knows that he himself must answer the question of what's right from both a worldly and a moral perspective. This at times will make his experience more exhilarating than that of other leaders, and at times more excruciating. But it will always be *his* experience—one for which he willingly takes responsibility. And what could be a greater or more meaningful adventure in leadership than that?

Index